CONTENTS

Introduction

Poverty is the one hundred and tenth volume in the **Issues** series. The aim of this series is to offer up-to-date information about important issues in our world.

Poverty looks at the problem of poverty in the UK, as well as internationally.

The information comes from a wide variety of sources and includes:
Government reports and statistics
Newspaper reports and features
Magazine articles and surveys
Website material
Literature from lobby groups
and charitable organisations.

It is hoped that, as you read about the many aspects of the issues explored in this book, you will critically evaluate the information presented. It is important that you decide whether you are being presented with facts or opinions. Does the writer give a biased or an unbiased report? If an opinion is being expressed, do you agree with the writer?

Poverty offers a useful starting-point for those who need convenient access to information about the many issues involved. However, it is only a starting-point. At the back of the book is a list of organisations which you may want to contact for further information.

*****

Poverty

ISSUES

Volume 110

Series Editor

Craig Donnellan

Assistant Editor

Lisa Firth

Independence
Educational Publishers
Cambridge

First published by Independence
PO Box 295
Cambridge CB1 3XP
England

British Library Cataloguing in Publication Data
Poverty – (Issues Series)
I. Donnellan, Craig II. Series
362.5

ISBN 1 86168 343 X

Printed in Great Britain
MWL Print Group Ltd

Layout by
Lisa Firth

Cover
The illustration on the front cover is by
Don Hatcher.

The facts about poverty in the UK

Information from Oxfam

How many people in the UK live in poverty?

Just under 1 in 4 people in the UK – or nearly 13 million people – live in poverty, according to the latest figures. This includes nearly 1 in 3 children (almost 4 million).

How were these figures calculated?

Poverty is measured here as below 60 per cent of contemporary median net disposable income in 2000/01. This is the 'poverty line' which has been accepted recently across the European Union to measure the extent of poverty in member states; it is not the same as a comprehensive definition of poverty, which includes many other dimensions. These figures look at incomes in Great Britain, after housing costs have been paid, and include the self-employed.

These figures don't mean very much by themselves – they only refer to low incomes relative to the rest of the population in the UK. They don't tell us much about the many different aspects of poverty and the way people experience it.

And they are a snapshot: they don't tell us how long people live in poverty.

What kinds of poverty are people living in?

One recent survey showed that about 6.5 million adults go without essential clothing, such as a warm waterproof coat, because of lack of money.

Over 10.5 million people live in financial insecurity: they can't afford to save, insure their house contents, or spend even small amounts on themselves. About 9.5 million can't afford adequate housing – heated, free from damp, and in a decent state of decoration. The crucial factor about these findings is that they are based on a survey of what the general population sees as necessities.

We also know what a dark shadow poverty casts, particularly over children's lives and their futures. Eighteen per cent of children go without two or more items that the majority of the population says are necessities, such as adequate clothing, toys, or three meals a day.

One in five non-working families on low or moderate incomes reported being unable to afford some basic food items on most days in 2000.

Children from poor homes are more likely to die as a baby or a child, and have lower life expectancy overall. They also have a greater likelihood of bad health, a greater risk of unemployment, and a lower chance of high educational achievement.

How long do people live in poverty for?

Poverty is likely to last longer for young children in particular. Overall, a recent survey found that about half of all individuals in the bottom fifth of income spent six or more years there out of ten.

Whilst people do move out of poverty, many do not move very far, and many more experience poverty sometimes.

Long-term poverty can eat away at people's savings and assets, leaving them more vulnerable: between 1979 and 1996, the number of households without any assets doubled to 1 in 10. It costs more to borrow money if you don't have much to begin with.

What kinds of people are more at risk?

Groups in the UK at greater risk of poverty include women, as well as children: nearly 1 in 4 women lived in poverty in 1999/2000, compared with 1 in 5 men – even before taking account of the 'hidden poverty' that may exist in households where income and other resources are not shared fairly.

Just under 1 in 4 people in the UK – or nearly 13 million people – live in poverty, according to the latest figures

Minority ethnic groups in the UK are often more vulnerable to poverty, in particular Pakistanis/Bangladeshis, more than two-thirds of whom were living in poverty in 2000/01. Some groups, such as asylum-seekers, also have to live on lower benefit levels.

Just under two-thirds of individuals in households containing adults of working age who had no paid work were living in poverty in 2000/01. And those in some regions were much more likely to be poor than those in other areas.

How many people in the UK are poor today compared to in the past?

Bigger percentages have been poor, and poverty has been more severe, in the past; but because of the larger population, more people live in poverty today measured by the standards of today.

How does poverty in the UK compare to poverty in other parts of the world?

Oxfam does not argue that the extent or depth of poverty in the UK is similar to that in developing countries.

But not all those living in the wealthier countries of the world fulfil the stereotype of the rich, privileged consumer. Some have been left behind, living in a parallel financial universe, often budgeting on a weekly

How do the UK public see poverty?

People living in poverty the world over often feel their voice is not heard and their dignity is not respected. The public in the UK has tended to be more judgemental about those living in poverty than people in many other countries – being more likely to say, for example, that poverty is due to 'laziness and lack of will-power', rather than to 'injustice in our society'.

They also often think that many people on benefit have enough money to live on; but when they are told the actual amounts (£53.95 per week for everything except housing costs and council tax for a single unemployed person, for example), they are more likely to acknowledge the existence of real poverty amongst this group.

Also, the experience of unemployment and poverty amongst friends and family tends to make people more likely to see poverty as primarily due to structural reasons, rather than the fault of individuals themselves.

cash basis, with no bank account, few local shops, and constantly juggling bills and debts.

Through their resilience, by making a supreme effort, and by learning from experience, people may get by. But every coping strategy has its costs. It is women who often take on the burden of managing the family budget, putting others' needs before their own and undermining their physical and mental health by doing so.

Oxfam also believes that the underlying causes of poverty, and the ways poverty affects people's lives, in the north and south of the world are very similar. Inequalities of power and wealth, and a lack of political will to put the fight against poverty top of the agenda, underpin the reality of continuing poverty in countries all over the world. And the way people living in poverty are treated by others, and often have no voice in decisions affecting their lives, is similar in the UK and elsewhere.

'Poverty strips you of your dignity.'
'Poverty affects your self-esteem, your confidence ... you feel totally powerless.'

The United Nations Development Programme sees poverty as a lack of capabilities to live a long, healthy and creative life, to be knowledgeable, and to enjoy a decent standard of living, dignity, self-respect, and the respect of others. It sees a 'life of respect and value' as a key aim of human development.

What is the government doing about it?

The prime minister has set out his commitment to ending child poverty in a generation. The numbers of those living in poverty have started to decline over recent years. But there is still some way to go to make a significant impact on the dramatic increase in poverty and inequality in the UK since the late 1970s.

As the Labour government has started to recognise, one of the crucial ingredients in tackling poverty is public support. Recognition and understanding amongst the general public of the seriousness of the problem, and a determination to do something about it, will be essential to a sustainable long-term strategy to eradicate poverty in the UK, as it is in all those countries in which Oxfam works.

■ The material on this page, from the website www.oxfam.org.uk, is reproduced with the permission of Oxfam GB, Oxfam House, John Smith Drive, Cowley, Oxford, OX4 2JY. UK Oxfam does not necessarily endorse any text or activities that accompany the materials.

© Oxfam

Poverty: the facts

Individuals – risk of falling below threshold of contemporary average [mean] income, 2003/04

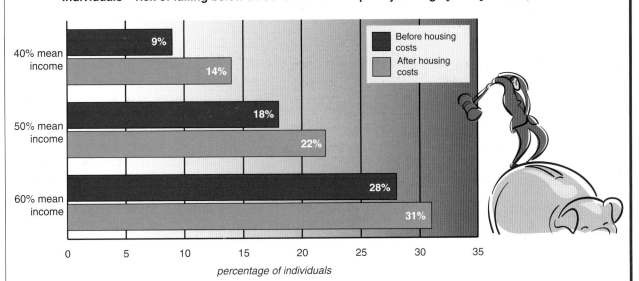

- **40% mean income:** Before housing costs 9%, After housing costs 14%
- **50% mean income:** Before housing costs 18%, After housing costs 22%
- **60% mean income:** Before housing costs 28%, After housing costs 31%

Legend:
- Before housing costs
- After housing costs

percentage of individuals (0, 5, 10, 15, 20, 25, 30, 35)

Source: Family Resources Survey, Great Britain. Crown copyright.

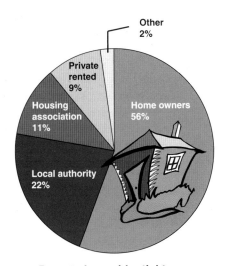

Poverty by residential types

- Home owners 56%
- Local authority 22%
- Housing association 11%
- Private rented 9%
- Other 2%

Source: Department for Work and Pensions

Spending on social welfare: government social spending as % of GDP

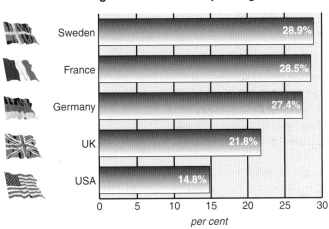

- Sweden 28.9%
- France 28.5%
- Germany 27.4%
- UK 21.8%
- USA 14.8%

per cent (0, 5, 10, 15, 20, 25, 30)

Source: Adapted from EQ5.1. Public social spending represents close to one-fifth of GDP on average, Society at a Glance: OECD Social Indicators 2005 Edition, © OECD 2005.

Example poverty lines in 2003/04

Family type	After housing costs			Before housing costs		
	50% median	60% median	70% median	50% median	60% median	70% median
Childless couple	£149	£178	£208	£168	£201	£235
Single individual	£82	£98	£114	£102	£123	£143
Couple with one child aged 8	£183	£219	£256	£206	£248	£289
Couple with two children aged 1 and 3	£186	£223	£260	£213	£256	£298
Lone parent with one child aged 8	£116	£139	£162	£141	£169	£197
Lone parent with two children aged 1 and 3	£119	£143	£167	£148	£177	£207

Source: Poverty and Inequality in Britain, 2005. Authors' calculations based on Family Resources Survey, 2003/04. © Institute for Fiscal Studies.

One in seven UK children live in poverty

By Sarah Left

Despite government efforts to improve the living conditions of poor children, the UK still has one of the highest rates of child poverty in the developed world, Unicef reported today.

Approximately one in seven children grow up in poverty in the UK, defined by Unicef as households with income below 50% of the national average. With 15.4% of British children falling into that category, the UK ranked seventh from bottom of a list of 24 industrialised nations studied by Unicef.

Children in the US and Mexico fared worst, with poverty rates of over 20%. Italy has the worst child poverty level in Europe, at 16.6%.

Denmark, Finland, Norway and Sweden had the lowest poverty levels, all below 5%.

Unicef said that, in the UK, the percentage of children in poverty was falling in response to government efforts to reach the children of poor families. However, in 17 of the countries studied, childhood poverty was getting worse, with between 40 million and 50 million children growing up in poverty in the world's richest countries.

'No matter which of the commonly used measures is applied, the rate of poverty among children has increased over the last decade,' a Unicef statement said.

In the UK, government campaigns have led to a 10% drop in child poverty, and the UK is on course for hitting targets of cutting child poverty by 25% by 2004/2005, according to the Unicef report, *Child Poverty in Rich Countries*.

Anna Wright, Unicef's project coordinator for the report, said the government was turning around the UK's appalling history on child poverty by targeting benefits specifically at low-income families. But she said the 25% of children the government is on target to raise out of poverty by this year will have been those living just below the poverty line. Reaching children stuck deeper in poverty will require increased government spending, she said.

'Government policy has had an impact and the UK is moving up the league table. But there needs to be higher benefits and more social spending and that's going to mean raising revenue through higher taxes,' Ms Wright said.

The UK government has set itself the goal of halving child poverty by 2010, and eliminating it by 2020.

> *Approximately one in seven children grow up in poverty in the UK, defined by Unicef as households with income below 50% of the national average*

A spokeswoman for the Department of Work and Pensions said: 'This report confirms that this government has succeeded in arresting and reversing the long-term trend of rising child poverty... However, we acknowledge there is still much more to be done.

'The government's strategy for tackling child poverty recognises that poverty is about more than just low income. It involves ensuring work for those who can and support for those who cannot; supporting parents in their parenting role; and delivering high quality public services,' she said.

The Unicef report found that Norway is the only country where child poverty can be described as 'very low and continuing to fall'.

Unicef noted that social trends, labour market conditions and government policies were the three

key determinants of child poverty rates. Higher government spending on family and social benefits was clearly associated with lower child poverty rates, Unicef found.

'On average, government interventions are found to reduce by 40% the rates of child poverty that would be expected to result from market forces alone,' the report said.

The report in particular contrasted government policy in France and the UK. Although the UK system favoured young children from low-income families while the French benefit system favoured no particular age group, the child poverty rate in the UK was double that of France.

'This points to a central dilemma: highly targeted social expenditures focus limited government resources on those most in need, but may lead to beneficiaries having less incentive to move from welfare to work. Benefits universally provided, though apparently more expensive, can avoid this poverty trap,' the report said.

With poverty rising across the majority of the countries studied, Unicef urged governments to set targets and timetables to maintain their focus. For most countries a realistic target would be 10%, or 5% for those where this has already been achieved, Unicef said.

1 March 2005

Child poverty

In their words

Michael's story

The best thing Michael's dad did for him was teach him how to break into cars. He showed him how to jump start them and drive them away. It was the only thing they ever did together. This was before he abandoned Michael's mother leaving her to cope with severe depression and a child, on very low income.

His mum relied on credit to buy things for the house. Over the years the family have always been in debt. When her new boyfriend moved into the family home she became very dependent on his earnings. Their relationship was stormy with bouts of drinking and domestic violence. Neither of the adults had much time for Michael and he was often sent to stay with different aunts and grandparents. He moved around between them and had no sense of stability.

This was the time Michael started getting into trouble. He was breaking into cars, rebelling at school and challenging his mother's authority. At 14 he was sent to a five-bedded children's unit. He had very little help with his school work and, despite being bright, was excluded from mainstream education.

Michael got involved in cannabis and heroin misuse. This made it difficult for him to hold down a college place and he moved on to a

Barnardo's
GIVING CHILDREN BACK THEIR FUTURE

training placement. It also put a serious strain on the relationship he had with his mum. As his habit increased he was spending up to £210 a week on heroin. He began to shoplift to obtain the money. He was charged and remanded to prison twice before being released and put on a two-year probation order.

Michael now attends a Barnardo's service for young offenders and is receiving help with his drug problem. He is now living in a bed and breakfast and is still in his training placement. He is looking forward to getting a decent job, meeting a girl and eventually having kids of his own. He says he'll be around for them in a way his own dad never was.

Julie's story

Julia Nixon is a lone parent with three children, Kerry aged 12, John aged 10 and Phillip aged 7. In answer to the question about whether it is a good area for children's activities Julia said, 'The only thing they have here is the sports centre. They get

bored going to the swings the whole time. Where there are bits of green grass they cannot play ball games.'

When we talked to Julia about the activities that the three children had been able to do in the summer holidays she said she had been aware of a summer playscheme but did not apply to it. She said, 'I do get the leaflets, but I didn't look into it as I'd have had to pay. It's all financial with three children on a budget. There's only so much you can do.'

Julia and the children had been on two outings with Barnardo's which were their only outings. Certainly the children had not had a chance of a holiday. 'I couldn't afford a holiday for the kids – we haven't had one for seven years.' When asked whether she had been able to take the children to the cinema Julia answered, 'that's what I call a luxury. We would have to cut back in the week to afford it.'

She also said that the children had done no sports activities in the summer holidays. Throughout the conversation Julia stressed the financial difficulty of organising activities for the summer holidays. She laid particular emphasis on the pressures of anticipating the new term and buying uniform. 'I try and buy certain things each week. Kerry's basic uniform cost me about £100 and that's without things for sports. John's winter coat cost me £35. The little bit of money you have left you have to keep back for what they need in the new term.'

Julia finished by saying, 'basically we just scrape by week by week. I'm in and out of debt with four catalogues and now I've got a bad credit rating. I've just finished paying off rent arrears.'

Breaking the cycle of child poverty

Information from Barnardo's

By Neera Sharma, Policy Officer

Poverty is the single greatest threat to the well-being of children in the UK.

More than one in four children lives in poverty.

In some regions, child poverty is even higher: rising to 54% in inner London.

But the starkest deprivation is found in tiny, almost hidden pockets: there are some wards in the UK where over 90% of children live in poverty.

Basic needs

Poverty is increasingly seen in relative terms: it is about not having access to what others in your society take for granted.

A third of children in poverty go without the meals, or toys, or the clothes that they need.

> *Poverty is increasingly seen in relative terms: it is about not having access to what others in your society take for granted*

For poor families, raising a child is not just about struggling to make ends meet; it's about struggling to give their child a chance to grow and thrive.

Serious threat

Growing up in poverty can affect every area of a child's development – social, educational and personal.

Living on a low income means that children's diet and health can suffer.

Poorer children are more likely to live in sub-standard housing and in areas with few shops or amenities, where children have little or no space to play safely.

Children from the bottom social class are four times more likely to die in an accident and have nearly twice the rate of long-standing illness than those living in households with high incomes.

They are also more likely to be smaller at birth and shorter in height.

Children who grow up in poverty are less likely to do well at school and have poorer school attendance records.

And the long-term effects of being brought up in poverty can be even starker.

As adults they are more likely to suffer ill-health, be unemployed or homeless. They are more likely to become involved in offending, drug and alcohol abuse. They are more likely to become involved in abusive relationships.

Persistent poverty

Once in poverty, children often stay in poverty well into adult life.

Recent research has found that most people remain in the same quarter of income distribution as their parents.

In fact, the chance of being better off than their parents has reduced for people who grew up in the 1980s and 1990s, compared with people who grew up in the 1960s and 1970s.

The key factors which suggest that children will fail to break free of the poverty cycle include: missing periods of school, being in care, being known to the police, misuse of drugs, teenage parenthood, and being out of education, employment or training between the ages of 16 and 18.

Targets

Ending child poverty by 2020 is one of the long-term goals of the government.

The government has concentrated on employment as the primary way out of poverty for families with children.

Tax credits have been introduced to supplement the incomes of working families.

The government can claim some success with child poverty, despite well-publicised difficulties with tax credit overpayment: overall, 700,000 children have been lifted out of poverty.

However, if the government wants to help the remaining children in poverty, more than tax credits are needed.

There are 600,000 children under three living in poverty and only 42,740 free or subsidised childcare places for disadvantaged families

The widespread availability of good quality childcare is crucial, both in enabling parents to work or train for jobs, and in giving children a head start in life.

Early years care and education is known to improve children's future educational achievement and health, but almost all childcare services for

children under three are private-sector arrangements for those whose parents can pay.

There are 600,000 children under three living in poverty and only 42,740 free or subsidised childcare places for disadvantaged families.

Work is not an option for all families, especially if they are caring for a disabled child or have health or disability problems themselves.

The children in these families grow up in persistent poverty and they must be the target of specific government policy if the goal of ending child poverty is to be realised.

Even where they are able to overcome the obstacles to work, the gains from earning for many families will be modest, and some families may even find themselves worse off after returning to work.

Work does not guarantee a route out of poverty.

Some of the initiatives set up to tackle exclusion are actually pushing those people not involved further towards the margins.

State benefit link

The Child Tax Credit established a guaranteed minimum income level for families in work, but there are no minimum levels for those on benefit.

For those who do not have paid work, income can be far below the poverty line.

Weekly income support for a couple with two children is around £178, compared with £253 in earnings at poverty level.

For a single parent with two children, income support is £147, compared with £175 in earnings at poverty level.

League tables on child poverty among developed nations show a clear relationship between levels of state benefits and the rate of child poverty.

All countries that have a high rate of social expenditure, such as Denmark, Finland and Sweden, have correspondingly low rates of child poverty.

However, many families even miss out on benefits they are entitled to because of the complexities of the system, language barriers and a lack of clear information.

What families need to get out of poverty are good local services, employment opportunities that support family life and an adequate income.

Child poverty is a social injustice, it is wasteful and it carries huge costs, both for the children involved and for society.

■ Published on the BBC News website, 25 July 2005. The above information is reprinted with kind permission from Barnardo's. Please visit www.barnardos.org.uk for more information or if you wish to write to them, please see page 41 for their address details.

© Barnardo's

Child poverty in the UK

Key facts

■ 3.5 million children are living in poverty in the UK.

■ The proportion of children living in poverty grew from 1 in 10 in 1979 to 1 in 3 in 1998. Today, 28 per cent of children in Britain are living in poverty.

■ Since 1999, when the current Government pledged to end child poverty, 700,000 children have been lifted out of poverty.

■ The UK has one of the worst rates of child poverty in the industrialised world.

■ The majority (52 per cent) of poor children live in a household where at least one adult works.

■ 45 per cent of poor children live in a household headed by a lone parent. The majority of poor children (55 per cent) live in a household headed by a couple.

■ The number of low-paid jobs has doubled since 1977 to over 6 million people, a fifth of the workforce.

The effects

■ 1 in 3 poor children do not have three meals a day.

■ 1 in 3 poor children miss out on toys, school trips and out-of-school activities.

■ 1 in 3 poor children lack adequate clothing, particularly shoes and winter coats.

Poverty and life chances

■ Poverty shortens lives. A boy in Manchester can expect to live seven years less than a boy in Barnet. A girl in Manchester can expect to live six years less than a girl in Kensington, Chelsea and Westminster.

■ Poor children are born too small; birthweight is on average 130 grams lower in children from social classes IV and V. Low birthweight is closely associated with infant death and chronic diseases in later life.

■ Poverty shapes children's development. Before reaching his or her second birthday, a child from a poorer family is already more likely to show a lower level of attainment than a child from a better-off family. By the age of six a less able child from a rich family is likely to have overtaken an able child born into a poor family.

■ Children growing up in poverty are more likely to leave school at 16 with fewer qualifications.

■ Children aged up to 14 from unskilled families are 5 times more likely to die in an accident than children from professional families, and 15 times more likely to die in a fire at home.

■ Girls who grow up in poverty are more likely to become mothers at a younger age.

■ The above information is reprinted with kind permission from the End Child Poverty Coalition. Visit www.ecpc.org.uk or see page 41 for more.

© End Child Poverty Coalition

Social exclusion

Breaking the cycle of disadvantage and social exclusion

This is a summary of the report published by the Social Exclusion Unit, on the government's agenda to break the cycle of disadvantage and provide opportunity for all. The agenda largely aims to tackle child poverty and long-term unemployment.

What is social exclusion?

Social exclusion is about more than income poverty. It is a term for what can happen when people or areas face a combination of linked problems such as unemployment, discrimination, poor skills, low incomes, poor housing, high crime, bad health and family breakdown. These problems are linked and mutually reinforcing so that they can create a vicious cycle in people's lives.

Social exclusion is often linked to the disadvantage children face at birth. It can be passed from generation to generation

---

Social exclusion is often linked to the disadvantage children face at birth. It can be passed from generation to generation. For instance, having parents who did not gain qualifications or who suffer from unemployment has an impact on a child's life and affects their opportunities in life.

The government's programme, which included setting up the Social Exclusion Unit, aims to break this cycle.

Initiatives implemented by the government

These include:
- Tackling key economic causes of social exclusion such as unemployment and poverty, particularly child and pensioner poverty.
- Promoting equal opportunities for all.
- Supporting communities particularly in deprived areas.
- Reintegrating some of those who have experienced more extreme forms of social exclusion, like rough sleeping.
- Improving access to advice and services.

Progress so far

- Reduction in child poverty – 700,000 fewer children living in poverty in 2002/2003 than in 1996/97.
- Sure Start Local Programmes – large-scale expansion of nursery education and childcare services.
- Reduction in pensioner poverty – 500,000 fewer pensioners living in relative poverty in 2002/3 than in 1997, and 1.8 million fewer living in absolute poverty.
- Reduction in unemployment – There are now 1.85 million more people in work than in 1997, and there have been faster than average increases in employment among some disadvantaged groups (e.g. lone parents, people with disabilities and those over 50 years old). Long-term unemployment amongst those aged 18-24 halved between 1997 and 2003.
- Educational attainment – Improvements for most ethnic minority groups, and progress in schools in the most disadvantaged local authority areas have been even faster than elsewhere.
- Homelessness – The number of homeless people sleeping rough has fallen by 70% and there has been a 99.3% decline in the use of Bed and Breakfast accommodation for housing homeless families with children since March 2002.
- Crime – Youth offending has reduced and juvenile reconviction rates fell by a fifth between 1997 and 2001. There has also been a reduction in crime and the fear of crime, including among older people.
- Teenage pregnancy – The conception rate for girls under 18 has fallen by 9.4%.

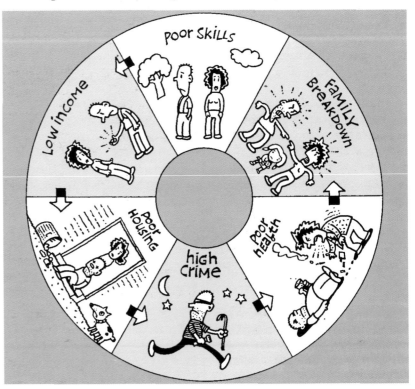

Remaining challenges

The government still has the following problems to meet:

- There are 5 key problems that continue to drive social exclusion, and that need to be made priorities over the next few years:
  → Low educational attainment among some groups
  → Economic inactivity and concentrations of unemployed
  → Health inequalities
  → Concentrations of crime and poor quality environments in some areas
  → Homelessness.
- Ensuring those people that have made progress do not slip back into a state of vulnerability.

There are now 500,000 fewer pensioners living in relative poverty in 2002/3 than in 1997, and 1.8 million fewer living in absolute poverty

---

- Constant monitoring and review of policies is needed to reduce the gaps between different social groups.
- To provide more support to children and families in the early years and at key transition points throughout their journey to adulthood.
- To improve service design and delivery to extend the reach of what works to the most disadvantaged groups.

There are currently 3 main groups of people for whom policies consistently seem less effective:

- People with physical or mental health problems.
- Those who lack skills or qualifications, both formal qualifications and broader basic and life skills.
- People from some ethnic minority groups, including asylum seekers and refugees.

What to expect in the future?

- Poverty and unemployment are declining and this trend looks set to continue into the next two decades.

- The ageing population is likely to present new risks for social exclusion.
- The number of single-person households is also increasing rapidly, and social isolation may also rise as a result.
- Inward migration looks set to continue. There exists a minority of unskilled migrants who face very poor prospects in the labour market and are of concern from a social exclusion perspective.
- The UK will continue to become more ethnically diverse and the pattern of persistent and multiple disadvantages among some ethnic groups may continue.
- Projections suggest that there is likely to be a continued growth in demand for skilled labour and therefore an increasing premium placed on formal qualifications.
- There is growing pressure on housing.

The government's next steps

- To sustain the progress already made.
- Provide more equal opportunities for people so that inherited disadvantage does not continue.
- Innovate in service design and delivery in order to benefit a greater number of multiply disadvantaged people.

- Anticipate and plan for the challenges and risks, which might be posed by future economic, technological and social trends.

- The above information is reprinted with kind permission from the Home Office. For more information please visit their website at www.crimereduction.gov.uk

© Crown copyright

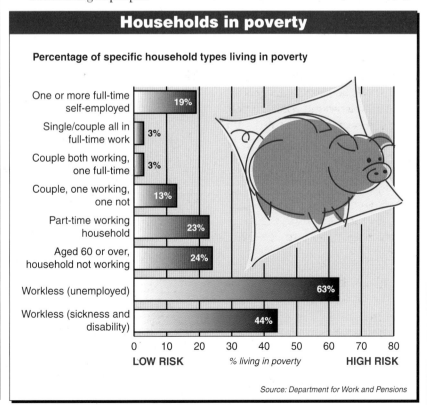

Households in poverty

Percentage of specific household types living in poverty

Household type	% living in poverty
One or more full-time self-employed	19%
Single/couple all in full-time work	3%
Couple both working, one full-time	3%
Couple, one working, one not	13%
Part-time working household	23%
Aged 60 or over, household not working	24%
Workless (unemployed)	63%
Workless (sickness and disability)	44%

0 10 20 30 40 50 60 70 80
LOW RISK   *% living in poverty*   **HIGH RISK**

Source: Department for Work and Pensions

Tackling child poverty

The government should do more to tackle child poverty in the UK, survey reveals

The public are aware of child poverty in the UK and believe that the government should do more to tackle the issue, according to research published by End Child Poverty today (16 February 2005).

Over half the respondents to an ICM survey for End Child Poverty estimated that 28 per cent of children were living in poverty in the UK or thought the proportion was even higher.

Only 4 per cent of the population believed there was no child poverty in the UK.

Women were more acutely aware of UK-wide child poverty with 67 per cent guessing the exact (or higher) level of poverty – compared to 42 per cent of men.

Ninety-three per cent of the population think that it is important to tackle child poverty in the UK with 74 per cent thinking it is very important to tackle the issue.

Eighty-five per cent said child poverty should be high on the government's agenda despite all the other issues facing the prime minister.

But the majority of the population (62 per cent) had no idea that the government had pledged to end child poverty in the UK by 2020.

End Child Poverty director Jonathan Stearn said:

'This is a call to action to the government. The public is aware of child poverty in the UK but have little idea that the government has pledged to do anything about it. It should tell the public loud and clear how it plans to end the blight of poverty for 3.6 million children.'

Through tax and benefit reforms the government has so far managed to lift a million children out of poverty.

But the End Child Poverty Coalition believes that the government will need to be even more determined if it is going to meet its next target of halving child poverty by 2010.

End Child Poverty has just published a 10-point charter, *Ten for a million*, supported by over 45 national organisations, showing the government how to remove another 1 million children from poverty and hit its 2010 target.

Notes

1. The survey was prepared for the End Child Poverty Coalition by ICM Research Ltd. ICM interviewed a random sample of 1,019 adults aged 18+ by telephone between 7th and 9th of January 2005. Interviews were conducted across the country and the results have been weighted to the profile of all adults. ICM is a member of the British Polling Council and abides by its rules. Further information can be found at www.icmresearch.co.uk

2. Asked to estimate the percentage of children in the UK living in poverty: 4 per cent said none, 27 per cent opted for 12 per cent, 28 per cent guessed the correct figure of 28 per cent, 14 per cent opted for 33 per cent of children in poverty, 9 per cent for 41 per cent and 50 per cent for 7 per cent.
16 February 2005

■ The above information is reprinted with kind permission from the End Child Poverty Coalition. Visit www.ecpc.org.uk for more or see page 41 for address details.
© *End Child Poverty Coalition*

UK tweens and teens among Europe's richest

Information from Datamonitor

London – A new report* from independent market analyst Datamonitor (DTM.L) reveals that UK Tweens** and Teenagers*** are Europe's richest. Annual income per capita reached £775 in 2003 – more than twice as much as their Spanish counterparts. The majority of this increased income comes from 'handouts' from parents rather than pocket money, which already accounts for 30% of their income. 'Parents are curtailing the growth in the pocket money that they give children, partly through fear of encouraging excessive consumerist behaviour at an early age but also increasingly because of fears regarding the consumption of unhealthy food and drinks,' comments Lawrence Gould, Consumer Markets Analyst at Datamonitor and author of the report. Their changing need states, growing incomes and shifting attitudes, as well as their increasing media savvy and sophistication makes them a challenging consumer group for marketers. Datamonitor forecasts that their annual income will increase by almost 10%, to £848 in 2008.

Notes

Tween and Teen Trends provides in-depth analysis of trends affecting Teen and Tween spending, including detailed information on levels of income and its sources. **Tweens are defined as consumers aged from 10 to 13 years. ***Teens are defined as consumers aged from 14 to 17 years.
21 January 2005

■ The above information is reprinted with kind permission from Datamonitor. Visit www.datamonitor.com for more information.
© *Datamonitor*

Poverty is damaging mothers and their babies

Information from the Child Poverty Action Group

New research published in Child Poverty Action Group's *Poverty Journal* conducted by Jonathan Bradshaw and Emese Mayhew from the University of York using the Millennium Cohort Study (MCS) demonstrates the damage done by poverty to mothers and their babies.

Bradshaw and Mayhew say that one in five of all babies in the Millennium Cohort Study were living in poverty.

Kate Green OBE said the research was shocking.

'The MCS shows that poverty in pregnancy or soon after childbirth has highly damaging consequences for mothers and their babies,' she said. 'Poverty in pregnancy continues to be associated with a much higher risk of low birth weight, maternal depression and a lower chance that the mother will try breastfeeding.'

Kate Green said that benefits levels were inadequate to protect mothers from poverty in pregnancy and after childbirth.

'Bradshaw and Mayhew show that the level of benefits for mothers on income support has not been increased in real terms since the end of the 1970s,' she said. 'The situation is worse if a single woman is pregnant when on income support – she will spend her pregnancy on as little as £44.50 a week, with serious consequences for her ability to afford a healthy diet essential in pregnancy.'

'Adult rates of income support need to be increased in line with those for children in order to improve child health indicators and raise more children out of poverty,' the authors of the report said.

15 July 2005

■ The above information is reprinted with kind permission from the Child Poverty Action Group. Visit www.cpag.org.uk for more or see page 41 for address details.

© *Child Poverty Action Group*

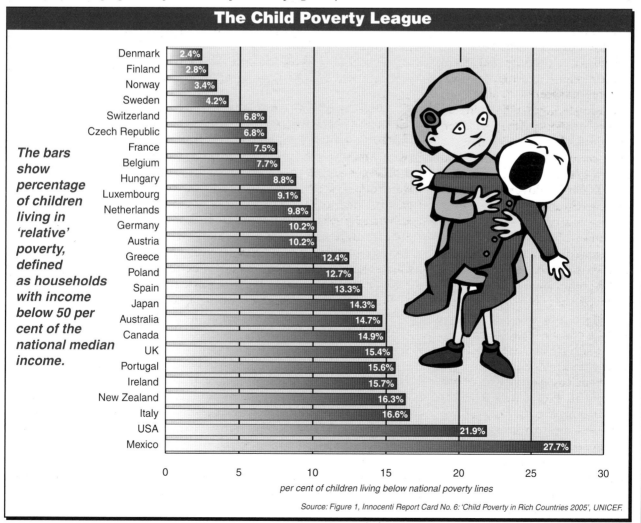

The Child Poverty League

The bars show percentage of children living in 'relative' poverty, defined as households with income below 50 per cent of the national median income.

Country	%
Denmark	2.4%
Finland	2.8%
Norway	3.4%
Sweden	4.2%
Switzerland	6.8%
Czech Republic	6.8%
France	7.5%
Belgium	7.7%
Hungary	8.8%
Luxembourg	9.1%
Netherlands	9.8%
Germany	10.2%
Austria	10.2%
Greece	12.4%
Poland	12.7%
Spain	13.3%
Japan	14.3%
Australia	14.7%
Canada	14.9%
UK	15.4%
Portugal	15.6%
Ireland	15.7%
New Zealand	16.3%
Italy	16.6%
USA	21.9%
Mexico	27.7%

per cent of children living below national poverty lines

Source: Figure 1, Innocenti Report Card No. 6: 'Child Poverty in Rich Countries 2005', UNICEF.

Households below average income

Key findings from the 2003/04 Households Below Average Income series

This article summarises key results from the Department for Work and Pensions and National Statistics publication, *Households Below Average Income 1994/5-2003/04*, which was published on 30 March 2005 (the full HBAI report can be downloaded at www.dwp.gov.uk/asd/hbai/hbai2004/contents.asp). The HBAI produces extensive data on trends over time and variations in risk in income poverty (henceforth termed poverty) and low-income. It also provides the data that underlines progress in the Govern-ment's pledge to eradicate child poverty by 2020, together with several Opportunity for All indi-cators. For consistency, this article uses after-housing-cost data only.

In 2003/04 about a fifth of people in Great Britain were poor, that is had an income below 60 per cent of the median income after adjustment for household size and composition. After having taken account of housing costs, children were especial-ly vulnerable, as shown by the risk of poverty in each age group:

- 21 per cent of all individuals;
- 28 per cent of children;
- 20 per cent of pensioners;
- 19 per cent of adults of working age.

Child poverty grew very rapidly in the 1980s, more slowly in the 1990s and has since begun to fall:

- 1979   14 per cent;
- 1994/95   31 per cent;
- 1996/97   33 per cent;
- 1998/99   33 per cent;
- 2002/03   28 per cent;
- 2003/04   28 per cent.

In terms of numbers, not per-centages:

- In 2003/04 3.5 million children were poor;
- Since 1996/97 the number of children who were poor has fallen from 4.2 million to 3.5 million – 700,000 fewer children in poverty;
- Between 2002/03 and 2003/04 the number of children in poverty fell by 100,000.

In 2003/04 the poverty line – the amount of money below which, after adjusting for size and composition of household and after housing costs, a family was categorised as poor – was as follows:

- £262 per week (£13,624 per year) for a couple with two children aged 5 and 11;
- £182 per week, (£9,464 per year) for a lone parent with two children aged 5 and 11.

Though the average risk of a child being poor in 2003/04 was 28 per cent, the risk of sub-groups of children being poor varies hugely by household characteristics and by geography. A few results illustrate the level of variation, and some of the groups of children most at risk:

- **Paid work** is very important in determining whether or not a child will be poor. 77 per cent of children in households with no adult in work are poor compared to 10 per cent of children in households with all adults in employment. Having a parent in employment is, however, no guarantee of not being poor. Having one, rather than two, earners; parental low pay and part-time work are each as-sociated with an increased risk of childhood poverty.
- **Ethnicity** is associated with differing risks of poverty, with Pakistani and Bangladeshi child-ren having an especially high risk of childhood poverty:
  → Pakistani/Bangladeshi children: 63 per cent;
  → Chinese or other ethnic group: 52 per cent;
  → Black or Black British: 49 per cent;
  → White: 25 per cent.
- **Housing** tenure is associated with varying risks of poverty. Families who own their homes (with or without a mortgage) tend to have a lower risk of child poverty than social or private renters:
  → Owner with a mortgage: 14 per cent;
  → Living in local authority accommodation: 56 per cent.
- **Household structure.** Children with lone parents face a much

Poverty Line

higher risk of poverty than children with coupled parents:

→ Couples: 21 per cent;

→ Lone parents: 48 per cent.

- **Disability** of both parent and child is associated with an increased risk of childhood poverty – and since the HBAI calculations take no account of the additional costs of disability, real living standards will be much worse than is apparent here:

  → No disabled adults: 26 per cent;

  → One or more disabled adults: 38 per cent;

  → One or more disabled children: 31 per cent.

- **Geography** is associated with variation in the risk of child poverty, with half of the children in inner London being poor:

  → Living in Northern Ireland: 25 per cent;

  → Living in Scotland: 25 per cent;

  → Living in Wales: 27 per cent;

  → Living in England: 28 per cent.

  Within England:

  → Living in the South East: 19 per cent;

  → Living in Eastern England: 22 per cent;

  → Living in the East Midlands: 25 per cent;

  → Living in the South West: 26 per cent;

  → Living in the North West and Merseyside: 29 per cent;

  → Living in Yorkshire and the Humber: 29 per cent;

  → Living in the North East: 30 per cent;

  → Living in the West Midlands: 32 per cent;

  → Living in Outer London: 34 per cent;

  → Living in Inner London: 51 per cent.

- Though **savings** might protect children against the effects of low income, those households with little or no savings are precisely those containing children at the highest risk of poverty – 49 per cent of children in households reporting no financial assets were in poverty.

- **Family size** and child poverty are associated – 51 per cent of children in families with four or more children were poor. So too is having very young children in families – 30 per cent of children in households containing a child under 5 were poor.

Children face a high risk of being **persistently poor** – that is, of growing up in households with incomes below 60 or 70 per cent of the median in at least three out of four years (data is for 1999-2002):

Geography is associated with variation in the risk of child poverty, with half of the children in inner London being poor

---

- 21 per cent of children were persistently poor, using the 60 per cent of median income threshold;

- 30 per cent of children were persistently poor, using a slightly higher 70 per cent of median income threshold;

- Children were more likely to be persistently poor on both the 60 and 70 per cent thresholds than either pensioners (17 per cent and 33 per cent; respectively) or working-age adults (9 per cent and 14 per cent).

As well as evidence on the risk of childhood poverty, the HBAI also has data on the **composition** of the group of children who are poor. Looking at both is essential since, though a group (for example, children in families with an adult in work) might appear to have a relatively low risk of poverty, if the group itself is a large one it may make up a substantial proportion of all children who are poor. Of the group of children who were poor in 2003/04:

- 42 per cent of poor children lived in lone-parent households and 58 per cent lived in a couple household;

- 48 per of poor children lived in workless households and 52 per cent lived in families with one or more parent in paid work;

- 37 per cent of poor children lived in owner-occupied accommodation and 47 per cent lived in social housing;

- 68 per cent of poor children lived in households with no savings and 89 per cent lived in households reporting less than £3,000;

- 44 per cent of poor children lived in households where the youngest child was under 5 years of age.

Income inequality. Though poverty has been falling in recent years, the difference between the incomes of the richest and the poorest remains substantial:

- The poorest fifth of the population received 5.9 per cent of total income; the richest fifth got 43.6 per cent (7.4 times as much);

- The poorest fifth had a median (the mid-point within the fifth) income of £128 per week; the richest fifth had a median income of £616 per week;

- The gap is shown to be even greater by dividing the population into tenths: the poorest tenth received 1.7 per cent of total income; the richest got 28.7 per cent (16.9 times as much);

- The poorest tenth of the population had a median income of just £88 per week, compared to the richest tenth with a median income of £789 per week.

March 2005

- The above information is reprinted with kind permission from the Child Poverty Action Group. Visit www.cpag.org.uk for more information or see page 41 for address details.

© *Child Poverty Action Group*

Rich-poor divide 'as wide as 60 years ago'

By Sarah Womack, Social Affairs Correspondent

The rich-poor divide in Britain is as great as ever, 60 years after the founding of the welfare state, according to new research that will make embarrassing reading for the Government.

The university study, which looked at social inequalities across the country, found that residential areas with the highest levels of poor health have the lowest numbers of doctors and dentists.

> *'Wide and persisting inequality is reflected in big differences between "rich" and "poor" areas in terms of housing, education and health care as well as economic wealth'*

Areas with the greatest number of young people with no qualifications also have the lowest numbers of teachers per head of the population. Areas with the highest number of qualified youngsters have four times the density of teachers.

The research also recorded a geographical divide based on access to cars, with about a million poor urban households having none. An equal number of households in the wealthy areas of west London has three or more cars.

The study was conducted at the universities of Sheffield, Bristol and Edinburgh, using data from the millennial census. Undertaken for the Joseph Rowntree Foundation – a respected social research charity – it was launched yesterday at the Royal Geographical Society's Annual Conference in London.

Prof Daniel Dorling, from the University of Leeds, said the report, *Life in Britain: Using millennial census data to understand poverty, inequality and place*, gave great insight into inequalities. 'Our research exploits data from the most detailed census information ever gathered on health, education, housing, employment and poverty.

'These are the aspects of British life that closely reflect the five "giant evils" of disease, ignorance, squalor, idleness and want that William Beveridge identified in his 1942 report leading to the creation of a welfare state.'

It was acutely disappointing, he said, to find that so many opportunities and resources still depended on where people lived. 'Wide and persisting inequality is reflected in big differences between "rich" and "poor" areas in terms of housing, education and health care as well as economic wealth.'

People in the poorest neighbourhoods with the greatest needs were often the least likely to have access to services and support that would help them 'improve their lives and life chances', he said.

Although the study found that living standards in Britain had risen since the welfare state was founded, it showed that the rich and poor still live in different worlds.

In England, Wales and Northern Ireland, young people are more likely to obtain good qualifications if their parents' generation, aged 40 to 45, is also well qualified.

Geographical location, as well as qualifications, can influence the chances of obtaining a well-paid job. High-status jobs are concentrated in London and the South-East. In areas where such jobs are relatively rare, there are higher proportions of people with good qualifications in low-status jobs.

Daily working hours are linked to geographical regions. In areas with low employment, people who have jobs are more likely to work longer hours than those with jobs in high employment areas. But this may affect their health, contributing to the cycle of inequality, because poorer people have less access to health care.

Dr Ben Wheeler, of the University of Sheffield, said he hoped the report would be used to highlight social problems that needed tackling. The authors hoped that it would 'add significantly' to the debate about the 'importance of tackling geographical as well as individual poverty'.

2 September 2005

UK rich not afraid of the red . . . ◆ ◆ ◆

. . . but North / South divide still flourishes. Information from Lloyds TSB

Northern Britain may be experiencing a boom in property prices akin to that traditionally seen in the South East, but the financial north / south divide is still alive and kicking, according to new research from the Lloyds TSB Plus Account.

The quarterly Urban Spenders survey tracks the spending habits of urbanites in the UK's top cities and reveals that the average UK current account balance is £1,650. However, regional differences soon become apparent, with the difference between the highest and lowest balance across the country standing at £879.

> **'Living in a city offers many temptations and it can be hard to keep a tight rein on your finances'**

Glasgow languishes at the bottom of the league, where residents have an average balance £1,221. Londoners top the table, as might be expected, with a balance of £2,279 but Bristolians are nipping at the capital's expensive heels with a balance of £1,730. Cardiff and Birmingham residents sit mid-table with balances of £1,527 and £1,516 respectively. Newcastle is the first northern city to appear in the league, where Geordie urban spenders have an average balance £1,510, beating Edinburgh (£1,481), Nottingham (£1,458), Liverpool (£1,446) and Manchester (£1,400).

Despite Londoners maintaining the highest current account balances, they also rack up the biggest overdrafts, with the average in the city being £961. It seems the higher an urban spender's account balance,

the higher their overdraft limit with the overdraft league table largely mirroring that for balances and once again it is metropolitan Glaswegians who sit firmly at the bottom of the table, with an average overdraft of £224.

Gordon Rankin, head of Lloyds TSB Current Accounts, comments: 'This Urban Spenders research shows us that whilst people might think that the more money you have the less likely you are to go into the red, this isn't so and certainly proves the old saying "the more you have the more you spend". People with money seem confident to utilise their overdraft and credit cards and it demonstrates these urbanites' modern approach to money management.'

City dwellers across the country show very different attitudes to cash. Given their place at the bottom of the balance and overdraft league, Glaswegians actually take out the most from ATMs each month – £409. This is £53 higher than Manchester

at £356, who come second in the league. Bristol and Cardiff, who scored highly in the balance and overdraft stakes, come at the bottom of the cash league, taking out on average £262 and £307 a month respectively.

Gordon Rankin concludes: 'Living in a city offers many temptations and it can be hard to keep a tight rein on your finances, but this research shows that Plus account customers are sensibly using the tools available to them to help them manage their cash. We pay interest of up to 4 per cent for Plus account customers who pay in £1,000 or more a month, which is one of the best rates around, so these Urban Spend-ers really are quids in.'
11 April 2005

■ The above information is reprinted with kind permission from Lloyds TSB. For more information visit www.lloydstsb.com

© *Lloyds TSB*

Income distribution of individuals

Quintile groups of individuals ranked by net equivalised household income, percentages, 2001/02 [1,2]

Region	Before housing costs					After housing costs				
	Bottom fifth	Next fifth	Middle fifth	Next fifth	Top fifth	Bottom fifth	Next fifth	Middle fifth	Next fifth	Top fifth
Great Britain	**20**	**20**	**20**	**20**	**20**	**20**	**20**	**20**	**20**	**20**
North East	22	25	21	19	12	20	25	22	20	13
North West	23	22	21	20	14	21	23	21	21	15
Yorkshire/Humber	23	23	23	17	14	22	24	23	18	14
East Midlands	22	22	21	22	14	20	22	22	20	16
West Midlands	22	21	23	20	15	21	21	23	20	15
East	15	18	20	23	24	16	17	19	23	24
London	19	16	15	18	32	24	14	15	18	29
South East	15	17	17	21	30	17	17	18	20	29
South West	19	21	22	20	18	19	21	22	20	18
England	*20*	*20*	*20*	*20*	*21*	*20*	*20*	*20*	*20*	*21*
Wales	*24*	*23*	*21*	*20*	*12*	*22*	*23*	*22*	*20*	*13*
Scotland	*22*	*20*	*20*	*21*	*17*	*19*	*21*	*20*	*22*	*19*

1. Total income of all members of the household after deductions of income tax and other contributions.
2. Figures for this year include the self-employed.

Source: Households Below Average Income, Department for Work and Pensions.

2m Britons are a week from the breadline

Nearly two million workers would be penniless within a week if they lost their jobs, according to a study published yesterday (4 January 2005).

Another six million would be on the breadline within a month, the insurer Prudential estimates.

The report highlights the lack of a savings culture among many Britons, with more than a million people hoping to achieve a financially secure future by marrying into money. A further 1.3 million are relying on a hefty inheritance from their parents.

The report found that 7 per cent would run out of money in a week if they lost their jobs, did not receive a redundancy payment and still had to pay regular expenses such as mortgage, rent or other bills and buy food.

Around four million (15 per cent) could manage for between a week and a month, while 30 per cent could cope for up to six months. A further 3.2 million would be penniless within a year and 1.6 million would last between one and two years.

Only 10 per cent, or 2.7 million, have the resources to survive longer than five years.

The research showed that it was not merely young workers living hand-to-mouth.

Only 30 per cent of those nearest to retirement (aged 55-64) said they could survive more than five years without dipping into their pension fund. Anthony Frost, of Prudential UK, said: 'The fact that over half of UK workers couldn't survive for six months after losing their jobs clearly demonstrates that the message about saving more isn't getting through.

'As a nation we are far too apathetic about money.

'The problem is that it's only when something unexpected crops up, such as losing your job or unplanned medical expenses, that the real and often dire nature of our financial situation is revealed.'

The research shows that 9 per cent of people hope to finance their long-term future by either finding a wealthy spouse or receiving an inheritance.

Mr Frost added: 'Lack of awareness, inertia and procrastination are all at work here.

'Worryingly, it seems that some are also living in hope by relying on little more than luck or a fairy godmother to finance their long-term future.'

■ This article first appeared in the *Daily Mail*, 5 January 2005.

© 2005 *Associated Newspapers Ltd*

The earnings gap

Rich earn 17 times as much as the poor

The gap between rich and poor is wider than ever, with the wealthiest 20 per cent of the population earning 17 times as much as much as the poorest 20 per cent.

But the gap narrows a little once taxes and benefits are taken into account, with the most well-off households bringing home four times as much as the poorest.

Figures from the Office for National Statistics show that more than 60 per cent of income from the bottom fifth of households was made up of cash benefits.

For the next worse-off group, benefits made up 37 per cent of household income.

Average household income for the top 20 per cent is £63,000 before tax and benefits, falling to £45,000 after. For the bottom 20 per cent it is £4,000, or £11,000 after tax and benefits.

Income support, child benefit, incapacity benefit and the state pension play the largest part in reducing income inequality.

The ONS pointed out that lower-income households also tend to receive more benefits in kind from the state, such as health and education services, since families and retired people are likely to be among the worst off.

Yet much of what the poor receive in benefits they have to pay back in taxes.

In 2003-2004, the wealthiest 20 per cent paid 25 per cent of their total income in direct taxes while the poorest paid just 10 per cent.

But the least well-off households actually pay a far greater proportion of their incomes in indirect taxes, such as VAT. They pay 28 per cent of their income back to the Government in indirect taxes. The richest pay 11 per cent.

The figures underscore Peter Mandelson's claim that Labour was 'intensely relaxed about people getting filthy rich.'

A study earlier this year found that under Labour the super-rich have become even wealthier. In the six years after 1997, the top 1 per cent of earners doubled their wealth to £797 billion. These people own 23 per cent of the nation's wealth, up from 20 per cent.

By contrast, the poorest 50 per cent saw their share of the nation's wealth shrink from 10 per cent in 1986 to 5 per cent in 2002.

■ By Jane Merrick, Political Reporter. This article first appeared in the *Daily Mail*, 8 July 2005.

© 2005 *Associated Newspapers Ltd*

Women and the poverty trap

Geethika Jayatilaka, of Fawcett, argues that the Government must do something to reduce the high incidence of poverty among women

Women are over-represented amongst the poor, globally. People don't seem to have a problem with this when they see pictures of women from faraway countries holding starving children to their breasts. But when these come from places closer to home, people are far less comfortable with the idea.

Lone parents today are the poorest group in society; two-thirds of children in one-parent families are poor, compared with one-quarter of children with two resident parents

Even the Government is not completely happy with the concept; they have made an admirable commitment to end child poverty within 20 years. However, they still talk about child poverty without discussing the seemingly obvious: that children are poor because their mothers are poor.

Obviously, not all women are poor, but women are overrepresented amongst the low paid (those on the National Minimum Wage) and those who live in poverty. The main reason that women are poor is because they continue to be the ones who care for the dependent: children, the elderly and the sick. This affects their ability to provide for themselves financially, in both the short and long term. The need for flexibility in work in order to cope with family responsibilities means putting up with the poorer pay. This forces women to either take part-time work and the 'top-up' state benefits available to them, or

leave work altogether (this is particularly true of lower-income mothers for whom the costs of childcare make it less worthwhile to carry on working).

Two groups of women are particularly likely to be poor: lone parents and pensioners. This is because both are disadvantaged by a system which fails to value women who care for others. It is traditionally assumed that women's incomes and work are unimportant because their partners will provide for them.

Lone parents today are the poorest group in society; two-thirds of children in one-parent families are poor, compared with one-quarter of children with two resident parents. The fact that the majority of lone parents are women is key to understanding why so many one-parent families are poor. Single mothers face the same issue that all working women face – the pay gap. The problem is intensified by having spent a couple of years working part-time, or out of the labour market altogether. For all lone parents, the lack of a second earner, or the potential for one, means that they will almost always be worse off than couples.

Women past the age of retirement, especially single older women, are particularly likely to be poor. The sad fact is that the pension system is an example of a policy made with men in mind, assuming that a long unbroken work history was the norm. Women were bolted on as an afterthought. It was taken for granted that women who did not work, or cared for family or friends instead of engaging in paid employment would themselves be taken care of in their old age by their husbands' pensions. However, husbands are not always for ever – through widowhood or divorce these women have been left without recompense for the years of valuable and important work they undertook.

Images of women's financial situations tend to be segmented into the career woman, the wife and mother, and the single parent. Policies are made to suit each of these neat individual categories. In reality, women occupy these categories simultaneously or move through these stages during their lifecycle. Politicians need to make policies which can accommodate this.

The need for women to have an independent income is not just about

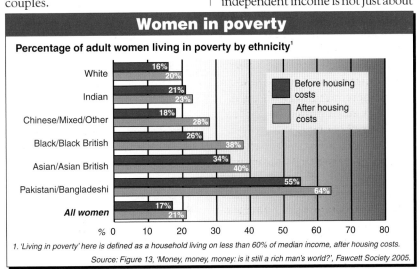

Women in poverty

Percentage of adult women living in poverty by ethnicity[1]

Ethnicity	Before housing costs	After housing costs
White	16%	20%
Indian	21%	23%
Chinese/Mixed/Other	18%	28%
Black/Black British	26%	38%
Asian/Asian British	34%	40%
Pakistani/Bangladeshi	55%	64%
All women	17%	21%

1. 'Living in poverty' here is defined as a household living on less than 60% of median income, after housing costs.

Source: Figure 13, 'Money, money, money: is it still a rich man's world?', Fawcett Society 2005.

equality – it is also about poverty. Demographics and society are changing. Men are no longer the sole providers. More women than ever will be lone parents, at least for part of their lives, and more families than ever rely on women's wages.

Government policies need to genuinely value caring, to ensure that women who care for their families, are not risking their financial well-being in the longer term. They need to encourage women to stay in the labour market by helping them combine work with family responsibilities.

Improving maternity leave, and providing good quality, affordable childcare will make it easier for women to spend time at home with their children, without compromising their ability to provide for themselves and their families – this goes for men too! The Government needs to encourage and allow men to take on their share of caring. In the longer term, this will help prevent the trauma of relationship break-downs being compounded by families falling into poverty, and should ensure that women do not end their lives poor as a result of a lifetime of caring.

■ The above information is re-printed with kind permission from iVillage Ltd. For more information please visit the iVillage website at www.ivillage.co.uk

What are benefits?

Information from askcab

What are benefits?
We use the term 'benefits' to describe any money that is given to us by the government. Benefits are paid to any member of the public, who may need extra money to help them meet the costs of everyday living.

What benefits are there?
Although there are many different types of benefit available, they can all be broken down into two main types. These are:
■ Means-tested benefits, and
■ Non-means-tested benefits.
Means-tested benefits will take into account your income (how much you get paid) and any savings that you may have. Means-tested benefits are then paid out, providing that your income and savings are sufficiently low enough.

Non-means-tested benefits do not rely on your income or savings, but your individual circumstances will affect whether your claim will be successful.

There are two main types of non-means-tested benefits. These are known as:
■ Contributory benefits, and
■ Non-contributory benefits.
You will become eligible for contributory benefits providing that you have made sufficient National Insurance contributions over a specific period of time.

Non-contributory benefits are paid for through the tax system, and as a result, will not rely on your contribution record.

So what are they for?
There are many different kinds of benefit available. Each one has been designed to pay out under specific circumstances. There are benefits available to cover:
■ Unemployment
■ Sickness
■ Disability
■ Housing issues
■ Pregnancy
■ Education
■ Raising a family
■ and many more.
It may even be that you are already eligible for some form of financial help because of your circumstances. If any of the above circumstances apply to your current situation, then you should enquire about claiming a benefit.

Who deals with benefit claims?
There are several government bodies throughout the country that deal with the distribution of certain benefits. These include the Inland Revenue, the Jobcentre plus agency, and local authorities (local councils).

The agency that you will need to contact will depend on the benefit that you are making a claim for. The A to Z of benefits section of the askcab site will tell you which agencies deal with a particular benefit, and will also provide you with information on how to apply.

It is important that you realise that the benefits system is a very complicated one, and if you find that you have trouble understanding your entitlement, or if you feel that you need help at any stage of your claim, then you should seek some advice.

If you do need any assistance, then please feel free to e-mail info@askcab.co.uk, or go to your nearest Citizens' Advice Bureau and speak to an adviser.

■ The above information is re-printed with kind permission from askcab. For more information, please visit www.askcab.co.uk

Older people and poverty

Help us eradicate the injustice of 2 million older people living in poverty

Facts on poverty

Too many older people are living on too little, forcing them to make life-inhibiting and sometimes life-threatening choices.

The UK is the fourth richest country in the world, yet thousands of its older citizens live without being able to meet basic needs, like enough food to eat or adequate heating for their homes.

The government has made a commitment to end child poverty by the end of 2020, but no such commitment has been made to the older community.

The basic state pension is £79.60 a week for a single person – £45 less than the Family Budget Unit says is adequate to live on.

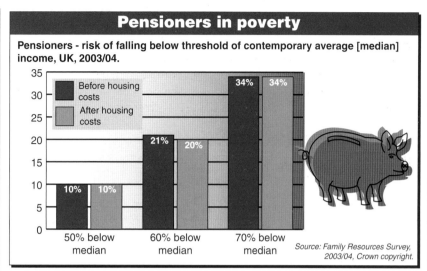

Pensioners in poverty

Pensioners - risk of falling below threshold of contemporary average [median] income, UK, 2003/04.

- Before housing costs
- After housing costs

	50% below median	60% below median	70% below median
Before housing costs	10%	21%	34%
After housing costs	10%	20%	34%

Source: Family Resources Survey, 2003/04, Crown copyright.

Why are so many older people in poverty?

- Many people never escape the cycle of poverty into which they were born. Children born into poor families often struggle in the education system and may well arrive at older age with a much lower income from which to derive a pension.
- 70 per cent of women have no private pension of their own, but outliving men means that they can face a longer period of poverty and ill health. Women are less likely to receive full benefits, however.
- Older people from ethnic minorities make up a disproportionate number of older people living in poverty. Government and agencies are failing to reach these groups.
- Older people with disabilities face twofold discrimination. They find it that much harder to get work, and information can be inaccessible due to sight, mobility or hearing impairment.

Pensions

More than 2 million people receiving a pension are still living below the poverty line. The current state pension is just £79.60 a week for a single person and £127.25 for a couple.

Research by the Family Budget Unit revealed a single pensioner needs up to £125 a week to pay for basic requirements like a healthy diet, adequate heating and transport.

Benefits take-up

- £2.5 billion of benefits that should rightfully go to older people went unclaimed in 2001-2002.
- One-third of pensioners entitled to claim Council Tax Benefit do not do so.
- Discrimination in the provision of disability benefits (people over 65 can't claim Disability Living Allowance, only the more limited Attendance Allowance) leaves many older people impoverished.

Council Tax

Council Tax is increasing at more than double the rate of pensions. While pensioners are means-tested for the benefits they receive, Council Tax is based on the value of property rather than the income or wealth of the people living there.

The result is that most pensioners spend large proportions of their pensions on Council Tax, leaving less cash for food, heating and doctor's bills. Confusing information and a lack of publicity means one-third of pensioners entitled to claim Council Tax relief do not do so.

Winter deaths

- Last winter 21,500 people over the age of 65 died as a direct result of the cold in England and Wales, according to the Office for National Statistics.
- Each winter over the last five years in England and Wales, between 20,000 and 50,000 people aged 65 and over have suffered avoidable winter deaths.
- The UK has a higher number of avoidable winter deaths than in comparable European countries. EU countries that experience more severe winters than the UK, such as Finland and Germany, have much lower levels of cold-related mortality.

Age discrimination

Too many older people are not viewed as being capable at work, or worthy as employees. Many are forced to leave the workforce prematurely, and are unable to find alternative work. This affects their future earnings, in terms of their pension, but also it affects their self-esteem and health.

Stop pensioner poverty

We believe poverty amongst older people can and should be eradicated.

Help the Aged is calling for:

- The take-up of benefits to be improved, by simplifying the system and improving publicity about what older people are entitled to.
- There should be a decent state pension for individuals of £105.45 a week and £160.95 for a couple. On a decent pension millions of older people would no longer need to claim benefits at all.
- The 25p-a-week increase on the basic weekly pension, at the age of 80 should be increased to an extra £5. Those over 80 are much more likely to be poor. They are often women, usually living on their own and often living with an illness or disability.
- An end to discrimination against the very poorest people. Currently those who work to supplement their pension income are taxed 40p for every £1 after the first £5 they earn. The 'earnings disregard' should be lifted to £75 a week to bring it in line with Carer's Allowance.
- Attendance Allowance lacks a component to help older people with disabilities to get around more easily. Yet people under 65 who become disabled receive this benefit.
- The installation and improvement of heating and insulation in older people's homes, to prevent them dying prematurely from cold because they can't afford to heat their homes.

- The above information is reprinted with kind permission from Help the Aged. Please visit their website at www.helptheaged.org.uk for more information about pensioner poverty and other issues affecting elderly people in the UK.

© Help the Aged

Government urged to back 'social tourism'

By Liza Ramrayka

Britain lags behind mainland Europe in helping families on low incomes to afford holidays, new research released today (8 February 2005) shows.

Holidays can improve physical and mental health and help families develop positive relationships. But around 25% of the British population does not take a holiday, largely due to low income, long-term illness, disability and family break-up.

> *Around 25% of the British population does not take a holiday, largely due to low income, long-term illness, disability and family break-up*

Research presented at a conference organised by charity the Family Holiday Association (FHA) suggested that the government has not prioritised this concept of 'social tourism' as its continental neighbours have done. The result is ad hoc statutory provision and reliance on voluntary sector initiatives.

The findings are part of a forthcoming report into UK family holiday policy and practice commissioned by the FHA from independent social policy research centre the Policy Research Bureau (PRB).

It highlighted practice in other parts of Europe, where governments have integrated 'social tourism' into their social welfare policies over the past 50 years, resulting in state-backed schemes to provide and promote affordable holidays and recreation.

In 2003, the Department for Work and Pensions recognised inability to go on holiday once a year as an indicator of social exclusion in measuring child poverty. The PRB said this sends 'a positive message', and suggested there may be opportunities within current legislation and policy for the government to promote social tourism. For example, the 2004 Children Act cites the UN Convention on the Rights of the Child requirement for leisure and recreational activities.

The Department for Culture, Media and Sport's 1999 tourism strategy also calls for broader access to tourism.

In France, around 6.3 million people last year benefited from a government-backed scheme for people on low incomes. Run by a national agency, the '*cheques-vacances*' (holiday cheques) scheme encourages employees to save part of their monthly salary, which is topped up (tax free) by their employer through the state-subsidised *cheques-vacances* scheme by between 20% to 80%. Vouchers can be used in over 135,000 outlets, including campsites, holiday parks and sports facilities.

In Belgium last year, the Flanders tourist office helped 10,000 disadvantaged people to take a break, backed by new regional assembly powers to tackle social disadvantage.

John McDonald, director at the FHA, would like to see the British government recognise the potential offered by such initiatives.

He said: 'Access to tourism in the UK has focused on disabled people, rather than other disadvantaged groups. We hope this starts a process of government working with the industry to include people on low incomes in holidays and leisure activities.'

8 February 2005

© Guardian Newspapers Limited 2005

Global poverty

Information from NetAid

What is Poverty?

There are plenty of statistics and data about global poverty – these are just a few:

- Each year, more than 8 million people around the world die because they are too poor to stay alive.
- Over 1 billion people – 1 in 6 people around the world – live in extreme poverty, defined as living on less than $1 a day.
- More than 800 million go hungry each day.
- Over 100 million primary school-age children cannot go to school.

Based on definitions established by the World Bank, nearly 3 billion people – half of the world's population – are considered poor. But poverty isn't simply a numbers game. It's about scores of men, women and children enduring unimaginable obstacles that keep them from fulfilling their most basic human rights and achieving their individual potentials.

When the United Nations created the Universal Declaration of Human Rights in 1948, signatories proclaimed that all people have the right to education, work, health and well-being. But today, millions around the world are too crippled by poverty to fulfil these basic rights. Millions continue to go hungry. Scores of children never step inside a classroom. Families watch their loved ones die from largely preventable causes because they do not have access to adequate medical care. In essence, poverty is a denial of human rights.

A global partnership to fight poverty

According to the United Nations and its affiliated development experts, an end to extreme poverty can be achieved. Effectively tackling global poverty demands a multi-pronged approach and there is no single cure-all. Issues of poverty are many and complex: initiatives must address interwoven but distinct issues such as children's rights, women's rights, epidemics such as HIV/AIDS, access to clean water and sanitation, and preservation of the world's natural resources – just to name a few.

The Millennium Development Goals, agreed to by the international community in 2000, represent an unprecedented opportunity for the world to usher in a new era of collaboration in fighting poverty. The Goals set forth concrete targets for significantly reducing extreme poverty and related ills by 2015. We are now one-third of the way to the deadline, and with just a decade to go, there is much work to be done.

Based on current trends, most developing countries will fail to meet the majority of the MDGs by 2015. The world has heralded 2005 as a milestone year in the fight against

Definitions of Poverty

- **Extreme (or absolute) poverty:** Living in extreme poverty (less than $1 a day) means not being able to afford the most basic necessitites to ensure survival. 8 million people a year die from absolute poverty.
- **Moderate poverty:** Moderate poverty, defined as earning about $1 to $2 a day, enables households to just barely meet their basic needs, but they still must forgo many of the things – education, health care – that many of us take for granted. The smallest misfortune (health issue, job loss, etc.) threatens survival.
- **Relative poverty:** Lastly, relative poverty means that a household has an income below the national average.

poverty, and it has even been given the moniker of 'The Year of Development'.

Many believe that achieving the MDGs must involve a real and measurable focus on Goal 8: partnerships for development. Governments working together with civil society, multilateral institutions and private sector entities is not just a nice idea, it is indeed what is needed to make poverty history.

Sources: Jeffrey Sachs, The End of Poverty (2005); World Bank; UN

- The above information is reprinted with kind permission from NetAid. For more information, please visit their website at www.netaid.org

© *NetAid*

Poverty

An overview

What is poverty?

According to a UN report released in February 2005, child poverty in the UK has fallen to 15 per cent of children. This is a big decrease from 33 per cent in 2002 (Department for Work and Pensions – see www.oxfamgb.org/ukpp/poverty/thefacts.htm). In Britain the poverty line is defined as half the national average wage – currently around £7,000. In the world's poorest countries earning this kind of wage would mean you were rich. As the Scottish Poverty Information Unit explains: 'Poverty is defined relative to the standards of living in a society at a specific time. People live in poverty when they are denied an income sufficient for their material needs and when these circumstances exclude them from taking part in activities which are an accepted part of daily life in that society.'

Whilst poverty is a major issue in Britain and may well affect the young people you work with, on a global scale most people in Britain are relatively rich in comparison with the rest of the world. According to the World Bank, one billion people live on less than one dollar (approx 60p) a day. The gap between the richest and the poorest is growing all the time. In the 1930s the ratio between the wealth of the world's developed countries and that of the world's developing countries was 2:1. In 2000 it was 40:1.

Why are people poor?

Poverty is a complex issue. Many factors, both global and local, contribute to poverty and they cannot all be considered here. However, many of the other issues addressed on the NYA (www.nya.org.uk) website have an impact on global poverty.

Harsh world trade rules and debt-relief conditions laid down by the World Bank and International Monetary Fund have led to poverty for many developing world farmers

The National Youth Agency

who were once affluent. For instance, coffee farmers can no longer protect their businesses using export taxes and the World Bank has encouraged the over-production of coffee world-wide, leading to a plummet in the buying price of coffee. Multi-nationals have further exploited this plummeting price by holding off from buying their coffee to make the price drop further. The push by super-markets in Britain to drive down prices and the development of multinational agribusiness has pushed many British farmers into poverty.

The privatisation of basic services in many parts of the world in the last decade has led to people having to pay much higher prices for basic services such as water. When Bolivia privatised its water services in 1999, bills were increased fourfold and suddenly accounted for more than half of the income of those living on the local minimum wage. Following massive street protests by ordinary

people, the water service was put back into the hands of the government and old prices were restored.

Women make up two-thirds of those living on less than one dollar a day (World Bank). They are most likely to work for nothing or to work for less than male counterparts doing the same job. In areas of the world which have become major tourist destinations, local populations often become impoverished as the money tourists spend goes to multi-nationals, not to the local community.

The poverty of the rich

'How many gleaming, cheerful, well-centred faces one sees among men and women whose livelihood is meagre; and how many clouded, petulant, craving faces among those who seem to have everything! Which of the two is poorer?' John F. Gardener.

Because a consumerist society only works when people continually buy, the role of advertising in consumerist societies is to make people think they always need something else to be happy. A constant barrage of new 'essential' items means that people who are rich by global standards continually think they are not. Instead of recognising their relative

wealth compared with many in developing countries, people are encouraged to think they are 'poor' unless they own the latest trainers or the newest hair styling product. Much of this advertising is aimed at young people in an attempt to make them consumers for life.

In a consumerist society the only valid wealth is economic wealth and wealth in possessions. As a result, many people in rich countries are economically rich, but increasingly poor in terms of culture, wealth and relationships. These forms of poverty can be seen in the lives of young people in Britain who are encouraged to spend increasing amounts of time doing part-time jobs to buy the latest fashion items or to spend time with their latest computer game or DVD instead of with friends and family.

In an increasingly globalised world where western media, and the consumerism they tend to promote,

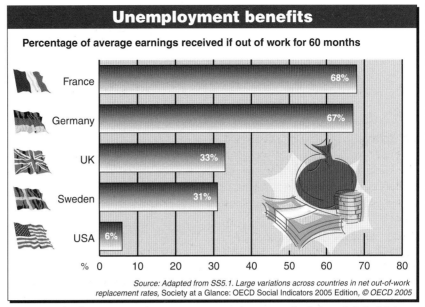

Unemployment benefits
Percentage of average earnings received if out of work for 60 months

Country	%
France	68%
Germany	67%
UK	33%
Sweden	31%
USA	6%

Source: Adapted from SS5.1. Large variations across countries in net out-of-work replacement rates, Society at a Glance: OECD Social Indicators 2005 Edition, © OECD 2005

increasingly dominates, the same is happening across the globe. The UN *World Youth Report 2003* tells the story of a subsistence community in Sudan. The village was the focus of an agricultural project which introduced money to the community. Many goods which were formally exchanged for other goods have become commodified. In the long term this has meant that young people are working longer and longer hours to earn the cash to buy these goods. They have lost time which they used to use to go to school and to socialise with the rest of the village. They have gained economic wealth, but they have few goods which they didn't have before because they cannot earn enough money from their land to enjoy the luxury items of consumerist society. In terms of time and enjoyment of their local culture they are far poorer than they were.

Eliminating poverty
'In order to satisfy the world's need for sanitation and food, all that is required is $13 billion ... This is equal to the total yearly expenditure on perfume in Europe.' http://homepages.uel.ac.uk/M.DeAngelis/ln1-science&values.pdf.

'Like slavery and apartheid, poverty is not natural. It is man-made and it can be overcome and eradicated by the actions of human beings. And overcoming poverty is not a gesture of charity. It is an act of justice. It is the protection of a fundamental human right, the right

to dignity and a decent life.' – Nelson Mandela, Trafalgar Square, February 2005.

In today's society poverty is not inevitable. We have the technology, knowledge and the resources to provide for the basic needs of all humanity. In 2000 the UN created Millennium Development Goals which aim to halve world poverty by 2015. Their scope includes hunger, disease, illiteracy, environmental damage, and halving the spread of HIV/AIDS by 2015. The goals also call for increased partnerships between developed and non-developed countries. Whilst the millennium goals require governments to take action to reduce world poverty, young people often have much more enthusiasm for reducing poverty than governments appear to!

There are a variety of ways in which young people can be involved in reducing worldwide and local poverty, from lobbying the government to do more to meet the millennium goals to fundraising for specific projects. If the young people you work with live in poverty themselves, then there will be many local-global connections to be made in your work. The resources listed on the NYA website will help young people get involved in reducing poverty.

- Information from the National Youth Agency. Visit www.nya.org.uk for more information or see page 41 for address details.

© *National Youth Agency*

World leaders 'could do more' to tackle poverty

Young people who responded to an online survey carried out by Plan said they believe world leaders could do more to tackle global poverty

■ **72% of the 10- to 17-year-olds, who took part in the 'Your Shout About Africa' survey, think world leaders could do more to tackle poverty worldwide**
■ **61% said they do not think politicians are doing enough to reduce poverty in sub-Saharan Africa, where $1 is the daily income for half of the continent's population**

The 'Your Shout About Africa' survey was conducted by Plan as a follow-up to the Young People's Commission for Africa, an educational initiative established by Plan in partnership with UK charity Gemin-i.org. The project brought hundreds of 11- to 17-year-olds together from 52 schools in Africa and the UK to discuss challenges facing young people in Africa, where nearly 50% of the population is aged between 5 and 24.

Out of the 637 young people who responded to the questionnaire 88.6% came from the UK whilst 11.4% respondents came from overseas.

The survey findings also revealed that:

■ Poverty and HIV/AIDS are seen as the biggest challenges facing young people in Africa (27.2% respondents said poverty was the biggest challenge whilst 26.5% said it was HIV/AIDS).
■ Tackling food shortages is regarded as a very important issue by 77% of respondents.
■ 73% of respondents believe it is important for politicians to work with young people to address these issues.
■ 62% of respondents think politicians are not doing enough to help reduce poverty in Africa.

The results of the survey are being launched on MAKE POVERTY HISTORY Children's Day and the C8, a UNICEF event supported by Plan and other charities from the MAKE POVERTY HISTORY coalition.

UNICEF's C8 will be the first ever children's alternative to the G8 that will bring young people from rich nations and poor countries together to lobby world leaders at the Summit.

Sixteen-year-old Chikondi Chiweza, a Young People's Commission for Africa representative from Malawi, is one of the African participants who'll be taking part in the C8. Commenting on the survey findings she says: 'Children of today will one day be the leaders of tomorrow. Young people make up nearly 50% of Africa's population, so when a decision is being made concerning them, who better to ask than the young people themselves?

'This is why youths should be consulted on issues that concern them e.g. education, HIV/AIDS because they will be able to provide fresh ideas.'

Marie Staunton, Chief Executive, Plan UK, says, 'Listening to children is a good investment for world leaders, not doing so is a missed opportunity. At Plan we believe that children are entitled to knowledge and understanding about the world they live in.

'We also believe that children are decision-makers of the future, that we should empower them to act as global citizens and consult them on what they think they can and should do to shape the world of the future in the interests of all.'

■ The above information is reprinted with kind permission from Plan-UK. Visit their website at www.plan-uk.org for more information or see page 41 for their contact details.

© Plan-UK

Natural resources are path out of poverty

Says the World Resources Report 2005

A report that challenges conventional approaches is released today (31 August 2005) at a critical moment in the battle against poverty. The report, *World Resources 2005: The Wealth of the Poor: Managing Ecosystems to Fight Poverty*, stresses the urgent need to look beyond aid projects, debt relief and trade reform and focus on local natural resources to address the crisis of poverty in all parts of the globe.

'Traditional assumptions about addressing poverty treat the environment almost as an afterthought,' said Jonathan Lash, President, World Resources Institute (WRI). 'This report addresses the stark reality of the poor: three-fourths of them live in rural areas; their environment is all they can depend on. Environmental resources are absolutely essential, rather than incidental, if we are to have any hope of meeting our goals of poverty reduction.'

The report finds that environmental organisations have not addressed poverty and development

groups have not considered the environment enough in the past. The model presented in the report details how natural resources – soils, forests, water, fisheries – managed at the local level are frequently the most effective means for the world's rural poor people to create wealth for themselves.

Dozens of case studies detailed within *World Resources 2005* demonstrate how local stewardship of nature can be a powerful means of fighting poverty. Control over restoring 700,000 local acres of denuded forests and grazing lands was given by the Tanzanian government to the Sukuma people and they now have higher household incomes, better diets, as well as increased populations of tree, bird and mammal species. Ucunivanua villagers in Fiji were given control by the government of clam beds and coastal waters, and because of local restrictions placed on fishing, mangrove lobster and harvestable clam populations have increased dramatically. In India,

community control over the watershed has led to a nearly sixfold increase in the cash value of crops grown in Darewadi Village.

'There are encouraging examples of ecosystems being managed for the long term to create wealth for poor communities, but there is still a huge job to do,' said Klaus Toepfer, Executive Director of the United Nations Environment Programme (UNEP). 'Natural resources can be properly used to greatly reduce poverty. The time has come to reverse the course of worsening diseases, depleted natural resources, political instability, inequality, and the social corrosion of angry generations that have no means to rise out of poverty.'

> *'Traditional assumptions about addressing poverty treat the environment almost as an afterthought'*

While globalisation has resulted in greater wealth for many people in urban areas throughout the developing world – such as parts of China and India – these gains have often bypassed rural areas, except in the rare exceptions detailed in the report. Nearly half of the world's six-billion people live on less than $2 per day. Three-quarters of those poor people live in rural areas. These rural households depend overwhelmingly on natural resources for their income. If these ecosystems become degraded, as many have over the past 50 years, they will never provide the fuel for economic development that will boost the rural poor beyond subsistence and into the mainstream of national economies.

'We need to stop thinking of the environment as a passive element. It is a fundamental part of community-based decision making,' said Ian Johnson, vice president of sustainable development, the World Bank. 'Unfortunately, the poor often lack legal rights to ecosystems and are excluded from decisions about ecosystem management. Without addressing these failures through changes in governance, there is little chance of using the economic potential of ecosystems to reduce rural poverty.'

The moment is critical in the battle against poverty because of converging current events. At the G-8 Summit in July 2005, British Prime Minister Tony Blair and other world leaders focused almost exclusively on the problems of global poverty. Prior to the G-8, the Millennium Ecosystem Assessment – a report by an international panel of 1,300 scientists – found how humans have modified and degraded the world's ecosystems in the past 50 years. In mid-September, heads of state at the UN Summit are expected to further review progress towards achieving the Millennium Development Goals.

'Community stewardship of local resources should be a critical element of any poverty-reduction model,' said Olav Kjørven, director, Energy and Environment Group, Bureau for Development Policy, United Nations Development Programme (UNDP). 'With greater income from the environment – call it "environmental income" – poor families experience better nutrition and health, and begin to accumulate wealth. In other words, they begin the journey out of poverty.'

World Resources 2005: The Wealth of the Poor: Managing Ecosystems to Fight Poverty is the 11th in a series of biennial reports on global environment and governance issues published since 1984. This particular report's focus on poverty issues follows upon conclusions from the previous two reports – the first was about ecosystems and the second was about governance. Since 1996, the series has been published jointly by the World Bank, the United Nations Development Programme, the

United Nations Environment Programme, and the World Resources Institute.
London and Washington, DC, 31 August 2005

■ The above information is from the World Bank. Visit http://web.worldbank.org for more information.

What do you know?

A quiz from Christian Aid

1. What percentage of the world's population lives on less than 50p/0.75 euros a day?
   A) Two per cent
   B) Seven per cent
   C) 20 per cent

2. The three richest people in the world have more wealth than how many of the world's poorest countries?
   A) Three
   B) 20
   C) 48

3. If the world's wealthiest countries gave a percentage of their income each year, the worst effects of poverty could be addressed. What percentage do they need to give?
   A) less than one per cent
   B) just over six per cent
   C) more than 15 per cent

4. How many people in sub-Saharan Africa are HIV-positive?
   A) 5 million
   B) 18 million
   C) 25 million

5. One of the Millennium Development Goals is that all children should have primary education by 2015. How many children currently do not go to primary school?
   A) 50 million
   B) 115 million
   C) 200 million

6. How many people in the world don't have access to clean water?
   A) 500 million
   B) 1.1 billion
   C) 2 billion

7. How many children die of preventable diseases each day?
   A) none
   B) 5,000
   C) 30,000

8. How many people in developing countries go to bed hungry each day?
   A) 799 million
   B) 546 million
   C) 427 million

9. Of the 1.3 billion people who live in extreme poverty, what percentage is female?
   A) 40 per cent
   B) 50 per cent
   C) 70 per cent

Answers: 1. C, 2. C, 3. A, 4. C, 5. B, 6. B, 7. C, 8. A, 9. C

■ The above information is reprinted with kind permission from Christian Aid. Visit www.christian-aid.org.uk for more information.

Frequently asked questions on world debt

Quick answers to some of the most frequently asked questions about where poor country debt came from and why we should cancel it, from the Jubilee Debt Campaign

Where did the debt come from?

Poor countries were lent money in the 1960s and 1970s. Some was for useful purposes, but much went to projects that did not benefit the country's people or that helped to prop up dictators. As interest rates shot up in the 1970s and 1980s, many countries ended up still owing more than the original loan, even after years of repayments. To make matters worse, lenders have attached damaging conditions to debt relief, for instance demanding privatisations which benefit big corporations in the rich world, or forcing cuts in public spending, meaning that some countries are prevented from employing teachers or buying basic medicines. People in the poor world are suffering both from repaying the debts and from these conditions.

Hasn't all poor country debt been cancelled?

No! At the beginning of 2005, only $49 billion of debt has been cancelled. Low-income countries still owe over $523 billion. Most cancellation so far has happened through the Heavily Indebted Poor Countries (HIPC) initiative, the current – grossly inadequate – international debt relief scheme. Almost $30 billion has so far been cancelled through HIPC since it started in 1996. But this falls short of what is needed – and what is possible.

Hasn't the UK cancelled all the debts owed to us?

The UK and a number of other rich governments have agreed to cancel the debts owed directly to them (bilateral debt) by the countries that have reached the first stage of the HIPC initiative (this is 27 countries so far.) The other indebted countries eligible for HIPC will also receive this cancellation when – and if – they reach this stage. Until then they must continue repaying their debts and the money will be held in trust.

What about debts being paid to the World Bank and IMF?

In 2004, thanks to vocal and determined campaigning, particularly through Jubilee Debt Campaign's Call for Change campaign, the UK government agreed to go further. It has promised to pay 100% of its share of the debt service being paid by poor countries to some multilateral institutions (the World Bank and the African Development Bank), for 10 years. The commitment covers the countries which have completed the final stage of the HIPC process (18 at present) as well as some other poor countries. In early 2005, Canada and the Netherlands announced similar initiatives. This is a welcome step, and a tribute to the efforts of campaigners. But the proposal does not contain everything that the Jubilee Debt Campaign is asking for, and is still very limited. In order to make a difference, all rich countries must agree to cancel 100% of multilateral debt, without attaching economic policy conditions. Jubilee Debt Campaign is asking supporters to send cards and emails to G7 Finance Ministers calling for 100% debt cancellation.

The UK and some other countries are suggesting that IMF gold reserves be used to fund cancellation of debts owed to the IMF. Jubilee Debt Campaign supports this proposal – but argues that if there is no agreement on using IMF gold, rich countries must still fund this cancellation, from their own resources.

What more could the UK do now?

Even if all G8 countries agree to cancel 100% of multilateral debt for a number of countries, there will still be more to do. The debt cancellation must be permanent – offering the fresh start demanded by the Jubilee movement – not just lasting until 2015 as the UK currently proposes.

The UK government, and all other lenders, must put an absolute end to the destructive and unjust conditions imposed by HIPC. All creditors must agree to debt cancellation for all countries that need it, including those poor countries currently receiving no debt relief, such as Bangladesh and Nigeria.

Giving aid, whilst simultaneously enforcing debt repayments, is to give with one hand whilst taking with the other

Doesn't corruption make debt cancellation pointless?

There is ample evidence to show that debt cancellation is an effective way to get money where it is needed. Tanzania and Uganda, for instance, have set up separate funds to channel money freed by debt relief towards poverty reduction. Mozambique has introduced a free immunisation programme for children. School fees for primary education have been abolished in Uganda, Malawi, Zambia and Tanzania. There is no evidence to suggest that debt cancellation is being used to fuel military expenditures.

Isn't trade the big issue now?

Poor countries need the opportunity to create wealth through fair access to trade. But they also need debt cancellation. If the debt is dropped, poor countries will have more money to spend on public services, including education and healthcare, as well as in infrastructure and equipment. Without this investment they will find it very hard to trade competitively in world markets. Debt cancellation and trade justice go hand in hand. Jubilee Debt Campaign is playing a central role in MAKE POVERTY HISTORY, which is calling for action on trade justice, debt and aid in 2005.

Isn't increased aid the answer?

Poor countries need a lot of investment. Giving aid, whilst simultaneously enforcing debt repay-

ments, is to give with one hand whilst taking with the other. In fact, debt cancellation is more reliable than aid, as it can't be switched off when the political climate changes. The reality is that poor countries need debt cancellation, increased aid and important improvements in how aid is delivered in order to meet the huge challenges they face.

How can we prevent another debt crisis in the long term?

In the longer term, governments must take action to ensure that we never return to a debt crisis like the one which has now been crushing poor countries for decades. It must be recognised that 'odious' debts,

incurred by oppressive regimes, should not be repaid. Debt audits or an open, just and impartial arbitration process are needed to judge which debts countries cannot and should not pay. The rich world should ensure that poor countries have sustainable financing to meet their needs, through an increase in aid and a bias towards giving grants not loans.

■ The above information is reprinted with kind permission from the Jubilee Debt Campaign. For more information please visit their website at www.jubileedebtcampaign.org.uk or see page 41 for their address details.
© *Jubilee Debt Campaign*

Millennium Development Goals

Information from Oxfam

In 1999, world leaders realised that none of the poverty reduction targets they had set for 2000 would be met. Embarrassed about this, they created a new set of aims for 2015, and coined them the Millennium Development Goals.

Achieving these eight global objectives could lift around 500 million people out of poverty. So what are they?

■ Reduce by half the number of people living on less than a dollar a day.
■ Achieve universal primary education.
■ Promote gender equality and empower women.
■ Reduce child mortality by two-thirds for all children aged under five.
■ Reduce by three-quarters the maternal mortality ratio.
■ Combat the spread of HIV / AIDS, malaria and other diseases.
■ Ensure worldwide environmental sustainability.
■ Develop a global partnership for development.

With only a decade left to achieve these goals, and progress to date painfully slow, Oxfam is taking action. We are campaigning for rich governments to take definite measures that will help to achieve them, such as increased aid, debt cancellation and fairer international trade. We are also working with groups in developing countries to make sure their governments are also doing what they can to meet the goals.

2005 is a critical year for the British government to show that it's serious about these targets and tackling poverty. All the opportunities are there: Britain is president of the EU, the G8 summit is held in Scotland, the UN will meet to discuss progress of the MDGs, and the WTO will conclude discussions on international trade rules. Oxfam will be lobbying the UK government and the G8 leaders, making sure that world leaders act on their commitments to eradicate world poverty.

■ The material on this page, from the website www.oxfam.org.uk, is reproduced with the permission of Oxfam GB, Oxfam House, John Smith Drive, Cowley, Oxford, OX4 2JY. UK Oxfam does not necessarily endorse any text or activities that accompany the materials.
© *Oxfam*

Millennium Development Goals: poverty and hunger

Information from the Department for International Development

Millennium Development Goal 1 – To eradicate extreme poverty and hunger

■ **Target 1: Halve, between 1990 and 2015, the proportion of people whose income is less than one dollar a day.**

Key messages
■ Extreme poverty is defined as having to live on less than $1 a day. If the proportion of people whose income is less than $1 a day was halved, it would reduce the number of people living in extreme poverty from 1.2 billion in 1990 to 890 million in 2015.
■ Globally, the number of people living in extreme poverty is falling, but there are large variations in progress between regions. Asia is making good progress, but there is little movement elsewhere and sub-Saharan Africa is going backwards.
■ Economic growth is a necessary condition for poverty reduction. The countries that have seen the greatest progress in income poverty reduction have been those with the strongest growth rates.

■ Growth is not just essential for reducing income poverty, but also for reaching the other Millennium Development Goal targets. Growth enables governments to fund more basic social services, it affects the extent of economic discrimination against women and also the extent to which poor people are either exploited or empowered in the economic, social and political arenas.

Facts and figures
■ In 1990, 28% of the developing country population lived in extreme poverty. By 2000, it had fallen to 22%.

If the proportion of people whose income is less than $1 a day was halved, it would reduce the number of people living in extreme poverty from 1.2 billion in 1990 to 890 million in 2015

■ East Asia has already cut its poverty rate in half and South Asia is making good progress.
■ In sub-Saharan Africa, the proportion in extreme poverty has risen slightly from 47% in 1990 to 49% in 2000.
■ In sub-Saharan Africa, the average per capita growth rate over the 1990s was -0.2%. In East Asia, it was 6.4%

Are we on track to meet the target?
Provided economic growth remains on track it is anticipated that 12.5% of the world's population will be in poverty in 2015, achieving the target.

Obstacles to improvement
Economic growth is a necessary condition for poverty reduction. However, economies can only thrive in countries where there is peace, stability and good governance. Beyond that, developing countries need to have more private investment from domestic and foreign sources and more diversity in their export and agricultural production to protect them against adverse price and weather shocks. They also need to have greater access to international markets – which means reducing or removing unfair tariffs and subsidies – and more, high-quality infrastructure for transport and communications.

Creating more wealth by encouraging economic growth is half of the equation. But poverty reduction depends upon wealth being shared out more fairly. The huge inequalities between the rich and poor in developing countries, where the vast majority of assets and income is concentrated in very few hands, is an enormous obstacle to reducing poverty.

Progress – What DFID is doing to help
DFID is trying to develop a better understanding of the linkages between growth and poverty reduction and identify ways to better promote the type of growth that the poor participate in and benefit from.

We are working with the International Monetary Fund (IMF) and the World Bank to improve understanding and analysis of the poverty and social impacts of major economic reforms, and to support better poverty monitoring.

DFID is providing money and expertise to support the development and implementation of country-led poverty reduction strategies in developing countries. This should lead to the creation of comprehensive and coherent poverty reduction plans that make the best use of the available government and donor resources.

What the international community is doing to help

Governments and multilateral institutions such as the World Health Organisation, OECD, the World Bank and the International Monetary Fund are working together to encourage economic growth and ensure that the benefits of this growth trickle down to the poor.

- **Target 2: To halve the proportion of people who suffer from hunger by 2015.**

Key messages

- The world already produces enough food, but the key to eradicating hunger is to ensure that ordinary people in the developing world can get access to it and that it's affordable. Poverty is the principal cause of hunger.
- Malnutrition remains a formidable obstacle to development. Efforts to reduce child mortality, improve educational attainment and enable people to invest in building a future for themselves are directly challenged by the persistence of hunger.
- DFID supports policies and programmes that will help make

815 million people still can't get the food they need for healthy, active lives. Most of these hungry people are women and children

food more affordable and available to poor people. When disaster strikes, DFID helps to get food to those who need it.

Facts and figures

- Over the past 40 years, global food production has doubled and food prices have halved to an all-time low.
- Bangladesh and India now produce enough food to feed their populations, but many people, particularly women, remain malnourished.
- 815 million people still can't get the food they need for healthy, active lives. Most of these hungry people are women and children.
- Two-thirds of the world's hungry people live in Asia, but Southern Africa has the highest proportion of people experiencing hunger.
- The number of hungry people in China, India, Thailand and Indonesia is falling, but in Bangladesh, Afghanistan, Nepal and sub-Saharan Africa, the numbers are actually going up.

- In sub-Saharan Africa, the number of people described as 'undernourished' rose by 50% from 125 million in 1980, to 186 million in 1997.
- In 2000, 38 million children in sub-Saharan Africa were malnourished, up from 22 million in 1980.
- In the developing world, two-thirds of child deaths are directly or indirectly attributable to malnutrition.

Are we on track to meet the target?

Some countries are making faster progress towards meeting the hunger target than others. China, India, Thailand and Indonesia have all reported a decrease in the number of undernourished people. However, in many other countries – including Bangladesh, Afghanistan, Nepal and many countries in Southern Africa – the situation is worsening. The main reasons for this slow progress include economic downturns, weak governance, HIV and AIDS and armed conflicts.

Obstacles to improvement

The main obstacle is poverty. Poor people can't get enough food, either by growing it or buying it. Introducing measures to reduce poverty will help to reduce hunger.

In the past, poverty reduction strategies have focused too much on treating the symptoms of hunger by providing food aid rather than dealing with the underlying causes. Hunger is inextricably linked to poverty. Instead of focusing on the production of food, the emphasis needs to be on its sustainability, accessibility and affordability.

The subsidies that the developing world pays to its own farmers, combined with the tariffs on exports from the developing world, make it very difficult for farmers in the developing world to get a fair price for their crops. If all tariffs were cut in half, the World Bank estimates that the economies of developing countries would benefit to the tune of £150 billion a year – three times what they receive in aid.

More and more forests and other natural habitats are being cleared to grow food. Poor management of the

environment and over-farming mean that great swathes of land will be unable to sustain crops in the future.

The causes of hunger and poverty are bound up with access to resources, markets, knowledge and political voice. Efforts to reduce hunger need to take this into account. Simply producing more food has not so far done enough to reduce hunger.

Progress – what DFID is doing to help

Since September 2001, DFID has committed more than £81 million to tackle the humanitarian crisis in Southern Africa and a further £21.3 million via the European Community. Much of this money has gone towards providing food aid in the short term and putting measures in place to provide food security in the longer term.

DFID is working closely with governments, the World Bank, the European Commission, the USA's Agency for International Develop-ment (USAID), other bilateral organisations and the UN to design and implement a food security programme for Southern Africa.

DFID has been actively pressing the European Commission to reduce, with a view to eventually eliminating, export subsidies in the World Trade Organisation in line with the commitments made at the Doha trade talks in November 2001.

DFID is supporting the creation of 'safety nets' to provide reliable help to the chronically food insecure. The aim is to provide an appropriate mix of cash, food and other support to help the poor build a more sustainable livelihood for themselves.

It also supports the sustainable livelihood approach, which recognises that poor people need access to natural, financial, physical, social and human resources to build a way of life that reliably delivers a decent standard of living. For more information about the sustainable livelihoods approach visit www.livelihoods.org.

DFID has also commissioned work on livelihoods, available from www.passlivelihoods.org.uk.

What the international community is doing

Since the World Food Summit in 2002, the international community has put more emphasis on developing practical and properly-targeted 'safety nets' in those countries where food aid is a regular requirement.

In 2005, the international community will take stock on progress towards the millennium goals. There is a task group for each millennium development goal. The hunger task force interim report can be found at: www.unmilleniumproject.org.

■ The above information is reprinted with kind permission from the Department for International Development. For more information please visit their website at www.dfid.gov.uk

© Crown copyright

Poverty and hunger

Information from People and the Planet

Some 1.2 billion people in Africa, Asia and Latin America are materially poor, with incomes of less than a dollar a day. Many are jobless, voiceless and powerless, either landless or have tiny plots. If they work in the informal economy they are often under-employed. Women and girls make up 70 per cent of their number. They are poorly educated and in poor health, their housing and shelter are meagre and they have few resources. Their life expectancy is short and declining in some countries.

According to the UN Food and Agriculture Organisation, 815 million people are chronically hungry

'Their destitution persists even though human conditions have improved more in the past century than in rest of history – global wealth, global connections and the technological capabilities have never been greater. But the distribution of these global gains is extraordinarily unequal' (World Bank).

■ Between 1987 and 1998, the number of the poor on the African continent increased from about 217 million to about 291 million. This means that 47 per cent of the population of sub-Saharan Africa are fully poor. (World Bank)

■ According to the United Nations Development Programme's *Human Development Report 1996*, the poor are generally worse off than 15 years ago, and, in some cases, poorer than they were 30 years ago. Globalisation has not helped them. Aid programmes designed for the poor have frequently done more to help the better-off.

■ The poverty of the poor means that most do not have enough land to grow the food they need, or the money to buy it. They may go hungry even when food is relatively plentiful in the area where they live. Nor do they generally have good access to social services such as education, reproductive health and family planning. According to the UN Food and Agriculture Organisation, 815 million people are chronically hungry.

Hunger

India has 208 million undernourished people, China 140 million, other Asia and Pacific countries 167 million, Sub-Saharan Africa 186 million, Latin America 55 million, Near East and North Africa, 36 million. While the largest number of chronically hungry people is in Asia, the depth of hunger is the greatest in Sub-Saharan Africa. Eighteen of the 23 countries facing the most severe problems in feeding their people are African. Afghanistan, Bangladesh, Haiti, Mongolia and North Korea make up the list.

The minimum number of kilocalories that a person needs varies between 1,710 and 1,960 per day.

Many of the chronically hungry people are short of more than 400 kilocalories a day.

Governments made a commitment at the 1996 World Food Summit to cut by half the number of chronically hungry people by 2015. Western governments have since cut their development aid to agriculture; in the 1990s this fell as a proportion of overall development assistance, 'from about 20 per cent in the late 1980s to about 12 per cent today...the declining support for agriculture is extremely damaging to efforts to reduce poverty and hunger', says a UN International Fund for Agricultural Development report.

■ The above information is reprinted with permission from Planet 21. Visit www.peopleandplanet.net or see page 41 for address details.

© *Planet 21*

Trading for justice

Information from Save the Children

Small farmers worldwide are forced to sell their produce for less than it cost to grow and harvest. This is because the international companies who buy most of it set the prices – and they want to keep their costs down to compete with each other. As a result, millions of small producers and their families live in poverty.

Fair trade companies offer a fair price for goods like cocoa and coffee to help farmers stay above the poverty line. More and more people in the UK are buying fair trade goods, but they still don't sell in massive amounts.

So, can fair trade make a difference? Here's what teenagers at a Save the Children residential in Oxford had to say…

'The principle's there, but the thing is it costs a lot more and people who aren't as well off as other people can't really afford to pay 50p or £1.20 for

Save the Children

chocolate and coffee when they can buy it cheaper.'
Sonia, 15, Nottingham

'Instead of just bringing out a new product which is able to give fair trade and good quality of life, maybe they should just rethink the rules so that all products have to do something towards making trade fair.'
Helen, 16, Somerset

'I'm not saying it's right – these big brand companies that have sweatshops and pay people peanuts make things affordable for people that aren't rich.'
Alicia, 15, Stockport

'For farmers in the third world, fair trade cuts out the middle man and they get more money for their produce and their work. And so their

families don't live in so much poverty. But it is expensive and there's still one in four people in Britain living in poverty.'
Mike, 14, Glastonbury

Facts about fair trade
■ UK sales of fair trade goods increased by 300 per cent between 1998 and 2003, reaching £100 million a year.

Fair trade companies offer a fair price for goods like cocoa and coffee

---

■ Fair trade coffee sales in the UK have reached almost £14 million a year. Total UK coffee sales are £730 million.
■ 500,000 farmers and workers throughout Latin America, the Caribbean, Africa benefit from UK fair trade sales.
■ The United Nations reckons that if trade rules were changed to help developing countries they could make up to $700 billion a year.

Sources: Save the Children, Fair Trade Foundation, www.realcoffee.co.uk, Trade Justice Movement.

■ The above information is reprinted with kind permission from Save the Children. Please visit www.savethechildren.org.uk for more information or see page 41.

© *Save the Children*

Fairtrade takes off in UK

The number of Fairtrade products available in Britain has rocketed from around 150 in 2003 to more than 700 today. The speed at which the range has diversified reveals a major shift in attitudes towards Fairtrade, the organisation says.

The latest figures include 500 retail products, 200 of which can also be used in the catering trade, and 200 items which are solely for catering. Fairtrade sales are growing by around 40 per cent a year, and sales for 2004 are expected to be over £130 million.

Britain has overtaken Switzerland to become the biggest Fairtrade market in the world

Britain has overtaken Switzerland to become the biggest Fairtrade market in the world, with coffee, bananas, tea and chocolate as still the most popular choices. Fairtrade wine and beer, roses and footballs were introduced last year, joining fruit juice, other fresh fruit, cocoa, sugar, snacks and honey.

The theme for this year's Fairtrade Fortnight which runs from 1 to 13 March [2005] is Check Out Fairtrade. This is a call to check out the Fairtrade Mark, a guarantee of a fair deal for growers in developing countries. It's also a call for consumers to check out the range of products now available.

Fairtrade composite products are a particular growth area – items such as muesli, strawberry jam, fresh fruit salads, flapjacks and chocolate chip cookies which include a percentage of Fairtrade ingredients. Fairtrade ingredients must be used wherever they are available and the minimum Fairtrade content is 20 per cent of the dry weight.

'There is a tremendous amount of choice when it comes to choosing Fairtrade products. People don't realise how many products there are and how quickly the range has diversified,' says Ian Bretman of the Fairtrade Foundation.

The guarantees behind the Fairtrade Mark are:
- Farmers receive a fair and stable price for their products.
- Farmers and plantation workers have the opportunity to improve their lives.
- Greater respect for the environment.
- Small-scale farmers gain a stronger position in world markets.
- A closer link between consumers and producers.

Tadesse Meskela, General Manager of Oromia Coffee Farmers' Co-operative Union in Ethiopia, explains: 'With Fairtrade coffee, farmers in Ethiopia are getting their deserved reward. Fairtrade is not just a selling and buying process, it is creating a global family.' Several other Fairtrade producers will also be in the UK, sharing their experiences and checking out their products on our shop shelves. They include Regina Joseph, a banana farmer from the Caribbean.

The list of suppliers of Fairtrade products can be found on the Fairtrade Foundation website.

- The above information is reprinted with permission from Planet 21. Visit www.peopleandplanet.net or see page 41 for address details.

© Planet 21

Awareness of Fairtrade

Fairtrade Foundation Awareness Research 2005

The latest MORI survey for the Fairtrade Foundation shows that one in every two adults in the UK now recognises the Fairtrade Mark. The study shows that 50% of people – half of the adult population – can now identify the certification mark, up from 25% in 2003 and 39% last year.

Alongside this, the proportion of adults correctly associating the green, black and blue Fairtrade symbol with 'Guarantees a better deal for third world producers' has risen significantly to 51%, up from 42% in 2004.

The Fairtrade Mark is reaching younger and more diverse audiences. The biggest age group recognising the Mark is now 25- to 34-year-olds (a 19-point increase to 55%) and this age group is also one of the most likely to buy Fairtrade products regularly.

The survey also shows that the majority of those buying Fairtrade are recent converts. More than half of Fairtrade buyers (53%) first bought a Fairtrade product in the past year, including 7% who first bought Fairtrade in the past three months. This figure equates to 3% of all adults in the UK buying at least one Fairtrade product over the past three months.

The latest figures show that an increasing number of people who recognise the Fairtrade Mark say they became aware of it through word of mouth – up from 16% in 2004 to 23% this year.

Furthermore, four out of five people who recognise the Mark say its independent guarantee of a fair deal for growers in developing countries is 'very' or 'fairly' important. The strongest feelings about the independent guarantee exist among 25- to 34-year-olds and those who regularly purchase Fairtrade products. Over half of these groups (52%) feel it is 'very' important.

25 May 2005

- The above information is reprinted with kind permission from MORI. Visit www.mori.com to view the technical details for this survey or for more information.

© MORI

Voters demand more action on world poverty

Information from Oxfam

A YouGov poll published today (24 April 2005) shows that 70 per cent of those eligible to vote in the UK General Election – equivalent to 30 million people – have taken action on global poverty since the last election. The British public overwhelmingly believes political parties must do more to end extreme poverty.

The poll, commissioned by the MAKE POVERTY HISTORY coalition, coincided with World Poverty Day on Sunday 24 April. All the UK's main political parties committed to use the day to campaign on their plans for tackling poverty in the developing world.

The poll reveals that 78 per cent of people want to see the main political parties do more on fighting global poverty. And 82 per cent believe that politicians need to respond as urgently to the number of children dying every day in Africa as they did to the Asia Tsunami. Two-thirds think that fighting poverty would do more to make the world a safer place than fighting wars can do.

MAKE POVERTY HISTORY is urging for action on trade justice, debt relief, and more and better aid at the 2005 G8 Summit, hosted by the British government in Gleneagles this summer.

MAKE POVERTY HISTORY spokesperson Alison Fenney said, 'Every single day, 30,000 children are dying as a result of extreme poverty. This poll tells us that the public are taking action on global poverty. Their campaigning work over the last five years has made global poverty an election issue. They want to see the next government do more on tackling the issues of Trade, Debt, and Aid. On World Poverty Day, political parties must respond on what they are going to do to meet these demands.'

On trade, 88 per cent of those polled believe that international trade rules should be rewritten to help people in poor countries to work their way out of poverty.

On debt, 75 per cent of people polled agreed that rich donors should cancel the unpayable debts of the poorest countries.

Every single day, 30,000 children are dying as a result of extreme poverty

---

On aid, 50 per cent of people polled wanted the UK to meet its commitment to giving 0.7 per cent of national income in development aid by 2010 or earlier. Currently, Labour and the Conservatives have plans to meet the target only by 2013, while the Liberal Democrats have set 2011 as their target. Almost one-in-four wants the UK to reach the figure by the end of next year.
24 April 2005

■ The material on this page, from the website www.oxfam.org.uk, is reproduced with the permission of Oxfam GB, Oxfam House, John Smith Drive, Cowley, Oxford, OX4 2JY. UK Oxfam does not necessarily endorse any text or activities that accompany the materials.

The rich-poor divide

Information from People and the Planet

In 1960, the per-capita gross domestic product (GDP) of the 20 richest countries was 18 times that of the 20 poorest countries. By 1995, the gap between the richest and poorest nations had more than doubled to 37 times.

- Of all high-income nations, the United States has the most unequal distribution of income, with over 30 per cent of income in the hands of the richest 10 per cent and only 1.8 per cent going to the poorest 10 per cent.
- In 2001 the average annual pay of US CEOs topped $11 million – some 350 times as much as the average US factory worker (who earned, on average $31,260).

Diseases of poverty and wealth

- Despite a slowdown in world population growth, the 49 poorest countries in the world still have populations that are increasing at an average of 2.4 per cent a year – nearly 10 times the annual growth in industrial nations.
- Infant mortality in low-income countries is 13 times greater than in high-income countries. In the 49 least-developed coun-tries in the world, women face a lifetime risk of death from pregnancy or childbirth that is more than 150 times greater than that for women in industrial nations.
- Lack of clean water or sanitation kills 1.7 million people each year – 90 per cent of them children.
- Sub-Saharan Africa is home to 70 per cent of the world's HIV-positive people. Only four per cent of people living with AIDS in low- and middle-income nations are receiving AIDS treatment.
- Europeans and Americans constitute just 28 per cent of the world population, but account for 42 per cent of deaths from cardiovascular diseases and cancers – diseases of affluence.

- Eighty-two per cent of the world's 1.1 billion smokers now live in developing countries.

Source: Vital Signs 2003, published by the Worldwatch Institute.

- The above information is reprinted with kind permission from Planet 21. For more information visit www.peopleandtheplanet.net or see page 41 for their address details.

© Planet 21

Children and poverty

One child dies every three seconds; 20 a minute; 1,200 an hour; 29,000 a day. At current rates of progress towards the Millennium Development Goal of a two-thirds reduction in child deaths by 2015, around 8 million children will still be dying that year, mainly due to hunger, neonatal disorders, diarrhoea, pneumonia and malaria. Sub-Saharan Africa will not achieve the Goal for almost 150 years.

In 1970, wealthy nations agreed to a goal of spending 0.7 per cent of their GNP on overseas development assistance (ODA). If the world's 23 largest donors actually delivered, ODA would be $165 billion a year – three times the current level and well above estimates of what is needed to achieve the Millennium Development Goals.

Today, over half the children in the developing world live without basic goods and services.

- One in six children is severely hungry; one in seven has no health care at all; one in five has no safe water and one in three has no toilet or sanitation facilities at home.
- Over 640 million children live in dwellings with mud floors or extreme overcrowding; and over 300 million children have no TV, radio, telephone or newspaper.
- Over 120 million children are shut out of primary schools, the majority of them girls.

Poverty undercuts a family or community's capacity to care for children. Globally:

- 180 million children work in the worst forms of child labour. · 1.2 million children are trafficked each year.
- 2 million children, mostly girls, are exploited in the sex industry.

Income inequalities have grown both across and within countries, despite an expanding global economy. In developing countries, children in the poorest quintile are more than twice as likely to die before age five as children in the richest quintile.

More than three-quarters of hungry people are in rural areas of developing countries. Children living in rural areas are twice as likely to be deprived of goods and services, and three times as likely not to attend school, as their peers in urban areas.

Child poverty has risen notably in richer countries. Only four developed countries – Canada, Norway, the United Kingdom and the United States – have fewer children living in low-income households than in the late 1980s. In 2000, only Finland, Norway and Sweden had child poverty rates below 5 per cent.

- The above information is reprinted with kind permission from UNICEF. Visit www.unicef.org for more information or see page 41 for details.

© UNICEF

Childhood under threat

Childhood is a brutal experience for half of world's children, UNICEF says – crucial years destroyed by poverty, conflict, and AIDS

'As children go, so go nations'

Despite the near-universal embrace of standards for protecting childhood, a new UNICEF report shows that more than half the world's children are suffering extreme deprivations from poverty, war and HIV/AIDS, conditions that are effectively denying children a childhood and holding back the development of nations.

Launching her 10th annual report on *The State of the World's Child-ren*, UNICEF Executive Director Carol Bellamy said more than 1 billion children are denied the healthy and protected upbringing promised by 1989's Convention on the Rights of the Child – the world's most widely adopted human rights treaty. The report stresses that the failure by governments to live up to the Convention's standards causes permanent damage to children and in turn blocks progress toward human rights and economic advancement.

'Too many governments are making informed, deliberate choices that actually hurt childhood,' Bellamy said in launching the report

at the London School of Economics. 'Poverty doesn't come from nowhere; war doesn't emerge from nothing; AIDS doesn't spread by choice of its own. These are our choices.

> *More than half the world's children are suffering extreme deprivations from poverty, war and HIV/AIDS, conditions that are effectively denying children a childhood*

'When half the world's children are growing up hungry and unhealthy, when schools have become targets and whole villages are being emptied by AIDS, we've failed to deliver on the promise of childhood,' Bellamy said.

The report – entitled *Childhood Under Threat* – examines three of the most widespread and devastating factors threatening childhood today: HIV/AIDS, conflict, and poverty.

Seven deadly deprivations

The report argues that children experience poverty differently from adults and that traditional income or consumption measurements do not capture how poverty actually impacts on childhood. It instead offers an analysis of the seven basic 'deprivations' that children do feel and which powerfully impact on their futures. Working with researchers at the London School of Economics and Bristol University, UNICEF concluded that more than half the children in the developing world are severely deprived of one or more of the goods and services essential to childhood.

- 640 million children do not have adequate shelter.
- 500 million children have no access to sanitation.
- 400 million children do not have access to safe water.
- 300 million children lack access to information (TV, radio or newspapers).
- 270 million children have no access to health care services.
- 140 million children, the majority of them girls, have never been to school.
- 90 million children are severely food deprived.

Even more disturbing is the fact that at least 700 million children suffer from at least two or more of the deprivations, the report states.

The report also makes clear that poverty is not exclusive to developing countries. In 11 of 15 industrialised nations for which comparable data are available, the proportion of children living in low-income households during the last decade has risen.

A growing war on childhood

Along with poor governance, extreme poverty is also among the central elements in the emergence of conflict, especially within countries, as armed factions vie for ill-managed national resources. The report notes that 55 of 59 armed conflicts that took place between 1990 and 2003 involved war within, rather than between, countries.

The impact on children has been high: nearly half of the 3.6 million people killed in war since 1990 have been children, according to the report. And children are no longer immune from being singled out as targets, a trend underscored by the September 2004 attack on schoolchildren in Beslan, Russian Federation.

The report also outlines where the world stands on a ten-point agenda to protect children from conflict, first enunciated by UNICEF in 1995. It examines trends in child soldiers, rape as a weapon of war, war crimes against children, and the damage caused by sanctions, among other issues, and finds that although some progress has been made it has been far from sufficient to ameliorate the impact of war on children's lives.

For example, hundreds of thousands of children are still recruited or abducted as soldiers, suffer sexual violence, are victims of landmines, are forced to witness violence and killing and are often orphaned by violence. In the 1990s, around 20 million children were forced by conflict to leave their homes.

Conflict also has a catastrophic impact on overall health conditions. In a typical five-year war, the under-five mortality rate increases by 13 per cent, the report states.

In 11 of 15 industrialised nations . . . the proportion of children living in low-income households during the last decade has risen

---

And with conflict aggravating existing poverty, the report emphasises the need for greater global attention and investment in post-conflict situations, to ensure a steady and stable transition to development.

When adults keep dying

The impact of HIV/AIDS on children is seen most dramatically in the wave of AIDS orphans that has now grown to 15 million worldwide.

The death of a parent pervades every aspect of a child's life, the report finds, from emotional well-being to physical security, mental development and overall health. But children suffer the pernicious effects of HIV/AIDS long before they are orphaned. Because of the financial pressures created by a caregiver's illness, many children whose families are affected by HIV/AIDS, especially girls, are forced to drop out of school in order to work or care for their families. They face an increased risk of engaging in hazardous labour and of being otherwise exploited.

HIV/AIDS is not only killing parents but is destroying the protective network of adults in children's lives. Many of the ailing and dying are teachers, health workers and other adults on whom children rely. And because AIDS prevalence grows in condensed pockets, once adults start dying the overall impact on surviving children in a community is devastating.

Because of the time lag between HIV infection and death from AIDS, the crisis will worsen for at least the next decade, even if new infections were to immediately stabilise or begin to fall. The report details the measures that nations must employ to prevent the spread of AIDS, keep adults living with HIV alive, and provide nurturing and care for children already orphaned.

Putting children first

The State of the World's Children argues that bridging the gap between the ideal childhood and the reality experienced by half the world's children is a matter of choice. It requires:

- Adopting a human rights-based approach to social and economic development, with a special emphasis on reaching the most vulnerable children.
- The adoption of socially responsible policies in all spheres of development that keep children specifically in mind.

- Increased investment in children by donors and governments, with national budgets monitored and analysed from the perspective of their impact on children.
- The commitment of individuals, families, businesses and communities to get involved and stay engaged in bettering the lives of children and to use their resources to promote and protect children's rights.

'The approval of the Convention on the Rights of the Child was our global moment of clarity that human progress can only really happen when every child has a healthy and protected childhood,' Bellamy said.

'But the quality of a child's life depends on decisions made every day in households, communities and in the halls of government. We must make those choices wisely, and with children's best interests in mind. If we fail to secure childhood, we will fail to reach our larger, global goals for human rights and economic development. As children go, so go nations. It's that simple.'
London, 9 December 2004

- The above information is reprinted with kind permission from UNICEF. For more information please visit their website at www.unicef.org, or if you wish to write to them see page 41 for their address details.

© UNICEF

Cost of school beyond reach of millions

Information from Save the Children

On the first day of the new school term, new research published by Save the Children reveals the prohibitive cost of school around the world, often beyond the reach of many parents.

In Liberia for example, sending one child to school costs half the average income of £62. This means sending two children would cost a full year's salary.

The research, *60 million girls*, launched in advance of next week's UN Summit, demonstrates that school fees are the biggest barrier to girls going to school. It shows that if fees were abolished in just 13 sub-Saharan countries an extra 4.5million children would immediately go to school. When Uganda abolished school fees in 1997 the number of girls in school more than doubled within three years.

As many governments do not have enough resources to financially support schools and abolish school fees, Save the Children calls on world leaders attending the UN Summit to commit to achieving the education Millennium Development Goals (MDGs) by ensuring all girls and boys complete a primary education by 2015.

A crucial first step to making this happen is for world leaders to enable school fees to be abolished urgently by 2006. With 100 million children still denied an education, 60 million of whom are girls, this is vital.

Fiona Weir, Director of Policy and Communications at Save the Children, said:

'Giving girls an education is one of the best ways to reduce poverty, malnutrition and HIV/AIDS but unless world leaders act now, they will condemn yet another generation to poverty. The UN Summit will be make or break. World leaders must show real commitment to abolishing school fees as a crucial step to making this a reality.'

2 September 2005

■ The above information is reprinted with kind permission from Save the Children. Visit www.savethechildren.org.uk for more information or if you wish to write to them, please see page 41 for their address details.

© *Save the Children*

Childhood deprivation in the developing world

Severe deprivation among children in the developing world, by region

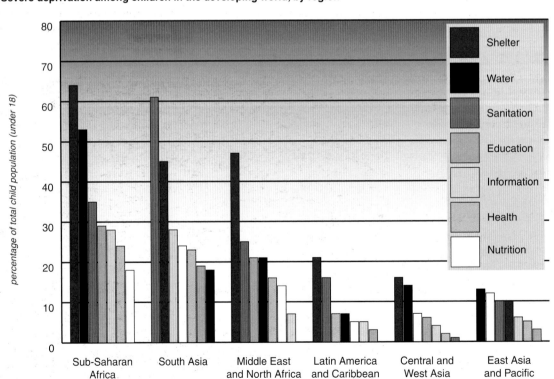

Age ranges: *Education: 7-18 years old; Information: over 3 years old; Nutrition: under 5 years old.*
Sources: *Gordon, David, et al., 'Child Poverty in the Developing World', The Policy Press, Bristol, UK, October 2003. Note: the data in the original study have been updated using Demographic and Health Surveys (DHS) and Multiple Indicator Cluster Surveys (MICS).*

Gender discrimination

Information from UNICEF

Poor access to education, food or health-care services has particular implications for women and children. The large disparities in most regions between the numbers of girls and boys who have never attended school are telling evidence of the discrimination that girls and women face. Gender discrimination is widely recognised as a major contributor to children living in poverty: how resources are earned, valued and distributed depends on power relationships between men and women within the household as well as within society.

Poverty denies children safety, dignity and protection

Each year, tens of millions of children are victims of exploitation, violence and abuse. Some are abducted from their homes and schools and recruited into armed forces. Some are trafficked and forced to work in prostitution and sweatshops, or needlessly deprived of parental care and forced into early marriage, or subjected to violence and abuse in the home, school and community. The effects of these abuses are far-reaching and enduring; they rob children of their childhood, preventing them from fulfilling anything close to their full potential.

How resources are earned, valued and distributed depends on power relationships between men and women within the household as well as within society

Many child protection abuses are linked to deeply entrenched material deprivations. One of the most obvious ways in which material poverty facilitates exploitation and abuse is through child labour.

unicef
United Nations Children's Fund

Material deprivation creates economic needs that can force even the most vulnerable children – such as those caught up in armed conflict, or orphaned or made vulnerable by HIV/AIDS – into hazardous labour, often at the expense of their education and recreation. Currently, 180 million children are engaged in the worst forms of child labour.

Material deprivation also makes children more vulnerable to trafficking and commercial sexual exploitation. An estimated 1.2 million children are trafficked every year; 2 million children, the majority of them girls, are sexually exploited in the multibillion-dollar commercial sex industry.

While poverty exacerbates child protection abuses, it is equally true that abuse often forces children into material deprivation, or exacerbates their existing poverty. Violence and abuse at home can force children onto the streets, where they are more likely to become entrenched in poverty. Discrimination can be an obstacle to learning at school and can cause children to drop out. Exploitation generates poverty by keeping children out of school, in poor health and subject to further psychological and physical abuse.

Currently, 180 million children are engaged in the worst forms of child labour

---

The Convention on the Rights of the Child makes it clear that it is the duty of governments and parents to provide the protective environment required to ensure that all children experience childhood in safety and dignity.

■ The above information is reprinted with kind permission from UNICEF. Visit www.unicef.org for more information or if you would like to write to them, please see page 41 for their address details.

© UNICEF

■ Just under 1 in 4 people in the UK – or nearly 13 million people – live in poverty, according to the latest figures. This includes nearly 1 in 3 children (almost 4 million). (page 1)

■ Poverty is measured here as below 60 per cent of contemporary median net disposable income in 2000/01. This is the 'poverty line'. (page 1)

■ Poverty is defined by Unicef as households with income below 50% of the national average. With 15.4% of British children falling into that category, the UK ranked seventh from bottom of a list of 24 industrialised nations studied by Unicef. (page 4)

■ Poverty is increasingly seen in relative terms: it is about not having access to what others in your society take for granted. A third of children in poverty go without the meals, or toys, or the clothes that they need. (page 6)

■ Social exclusion is a term for what can happen when people or areas face a combination of linked problems such as unemployment, discrimination, poor skills, low incomes, poor housing, high crime, bad health and family breakdown. (page 8)

■ Ninety-three per cent of the population think that it is important to tackle child poverty in the UK with 74 per cent thinking it is very important to tackle the issue. (page 10)

■ Ethnicity is associated with differing risks of poverty, with Pakistani and Bangladeshi children having an especially high risk of childhood poverty. (page 12)

■ Of the group of children who were poor in 2003/04, 42 per cent lived in lone-parent households and 58 per cent lived in a couple household. (page 13)

■ The rich-poor divide in Britain is as great as ever, 60 years after the founding of the welfare state, according to new research. (page 14)

■ The gap between rich and poor is wider than ever, with the wealthiest 20 per cent of the population earning 17 times as much as much as the poorest 20. (page 16)

■ Women are over-represented amongst the low paid (those on the National Minimum Wage) and those who live in poverty. (page 17)

■ More than 2 million people receiving a pension are still living below the poverty line. The current state pension is just £79.60 a week for a single person and £127.25 for a couple. (page 19)

■ Over 1 billion people – 1 in 6 people around the world – live in extreme poverty, defined as living on less than $1 a day. (page 21)

■ The international community has agreed upon a framework, the Millennium Development Goals, for reducing poverty in half by 2015. (page 23)

■ 72% of the 10- to 17-year-olds, who took part in the 'Your Shout About Africa' survey, think world leaders could do more to tackle poverty worldwide. 61% said they do not think politicians are doing enough to reduce poverty in sub-Saharan Africa, where $1 is the daily income for half of the continent's population. (page 24)

■ 20% of the world's population lives on less than 50p a day. (page 26)

■ At the beginning of 2005, only $49 billion of debt has been cancelled. Low-income countries still owe over $523 billion. (page 27)

■ In 1990, 28% of the developing country population lived in extreme poverty. By 2000, it had fallen to 22%. (page 29)

■ 815 million people still can't get the food they need for healthy, active lives. Most of these hungry people are women and children. (page 30)

■ Between 1987 and 1998, the number of poor on the African continent increased from about 217 million to about 291 million. This means that 47% of the population of sub-Saharan Africa are fully poor. (page 31)

■ Fair trade companies offer a fair price for goods like cocoa and coffee to help farmers stay above the poverty line. More and more people in the UK are buying fair trade goods. (page 32)

■ 78 per cent of people want to see the main political parties do more on fighting global poverty. (page 34)

■ One child dies every three seconds; 20 a minute; 1,200 an hour; 29,000 a day. (page 35)

■ Infant mortality in low-income countries is 13 times greater than in high-income countries. (page 35)

■ Material deprivation also makes children more vulnerable to trafficking and commercial sexual exploitation. An estimated 1.2 million children are trafficked every year; 2 million children, the majority of them girls, are sexually exploited in the multibillion-dollar commercial sex industry. (page 39)

You might like to contact the following organisations for further information. Due to the increasing cost of postage, many organisations cannot respond to enquiries unless they receive a stamped, addressed envelope.

Barnardo's
Tanners Lane
Barkingside
ILFORD
Essex IG6 1QG
Tel: 020 8550 8822
Email:
media.team@barnardos.org.uk
Website: www.barnardos.org.uk
Barnardo's works with over 47,000 children, young people and their families in more than 300 projects across the country. This includes work with children affected by today's most urgent issues: homelessness, poverty, disability, bereavement and abuse.

Child Poverty Action Group (CPAG)
94 White Lion Street
LONDON N1 9PF
Tel: 020 7837 7979
Email: staff@cpag.org.uk
Website: www.cpag.org.uk
The Child Action Poverty Group (CPAG Ltd) is a national charity which has been in the front line of the fight against poverty for over 30 years. CPAG campaigns for improvements in both benefits and other policies to eradicate the injustice of poverty.

End Child Poverty Coalition
10 Wakley Street
LONDON EC1 7QE
Tel: 020 7843 1914
Email: info@ecpc.org.uk
Website: www.ecpc.org.uk
12 leading charities working with children and families joined forces to set up the End Child Poverty Coalition. We have received wide support from a broad range of organisations, some of whom joined us at the official launch in April 2001. Our goal is simple – to eradicate child poverty.

Jubilee Debt Campaign
The Graystone Centre
28 Charles Square
LONDON N1 6HT
Tel: 020 7324 4722
Email:
info@jubileedebtcampaign.org.uk
Website:
www.jubileedebtcampaign.org.uk
Jubilee Debt Campaign demand an end to the scandal of poor countries paying money to the rich world. We are calling for 100% cancellation of unpayable and unfair poor country debts.

The National Youth Agency (NYA)
Eastgate House
19-23 Humberstone Road
LEICESTER LE5 3GJ
Tel: 0116 242 7350
Email:
youthinformation@nya.org.uk
nya@nya.org.uk
Website:
www.youthinformation.com
www.nya.org.uk
The National Youth Agency aims to advance youth work to promote young people's personal and social development, and their voice, influence and place in society.

Oxfam
Oxfam House
John Smith Drive
OXFORD OX4 2JY
Tel: 01865 473727
Email: enquiries@oxfam.org.uk
Website: www.oxfam.org.uk
Oxfam GB is a development, relief, and campaigning organisation dedicated to finding lasting solutions to poverty and suffering around the world.

Plan-UK
2nd Floor
5-6 Underhill Street
LONDON NW1 7HS
Tel: 020 7485 6612
Email: mail@plan-international.org
Website: www.plan-uk.org
Plan is an international, humanitarian, child-focused development organisation with no religious, political or governmental affiliations. We work with children, their families and communities in developing countries, helping to implement projects in health, education, water and sanitation, and income-generation.

Planet 21
60 Twisden Road
LONDON NW5 1DN
Tel: 020 7485 3136
Email: planet21@totalise.co.uk
Website:
www.peopleandplanet.net
peopleandplanet.net provides a global review and internet gateway into the issues of population, poverty, health, consumption and the environment. It is published by Planet 21, an independent non-profit company and a registered British charity recognised by the United Nations.

Save the Children
1 St John's Lane
LONDON EC1M 4AR
Tel: 0207 012 6400
Email: enquiries@scfuk.org.uk
Website:
www.savethechildren.org.uk
Save the Children is the leading UK charity working to create a better world for children. We work in 70 countries helping children in the world's most impoverished communities.

United Kingdom Committee for UNICEF
Africa House
64-78 Kingsway
LONDON WC2B 6NB
Tel: 0207 405 5592
Email: info@unicef.org.uk
Website: www.unicef.org.uk
UNICEF, the United Nations Children's Fund, is a global champion for children's rights which makes a lasting difference by working with communities and influencing governments.

INDEX

ACKNOWLEDGEMENTS

The publisher is grateful for permission to reproduce the following material.

While every care has been taken to trace and acknowledge copyright, the publisher tenders its apology for any accidental infringement or where copyright has proved untraceable. The publisher would be pleased to come to a suitable arrangement in any such case with the rightful owner.

Chapter One: Poverty in the UK

The facts about poverty in the UK, © Oxfam GB, *One in seven UK children live in poverty*, © Guardian Newspapers Ltd 2005, *Child poverty*, © Barnardo's 2005, *Breaking the cycle of child poverty*, © Barnardo's, *Child poverty in the UK*, © End Child Poverty Coalition, *Social exclusion*, © Crown copyright is reproduced with the permission of Her Majesty's Stationery Office, *Tackling child poverty*, © End Child Poverty Coalition, *UK tweens and teens among Europe's richest*, © Datamonitor, *Poverty is damaging mothers and their babies*, © Child Poverty Action Group, *Households below average income*, © Child Poverty Action Group, *Rich-poor divide 'as wide as 60 years ago'*, © Telegraph Group Limited 2005, *UK rich not afraid of the red . . .*, © Lloyds TSB, *2m Britons are a week from the breadline*, © 2005 Associated Newspapers Ltd, *The earnings gap*, © 2005 Associated Newspapers Ltd, *Women and the poverty trap*, © iVillage Ltd, *What are benefits?*, © askcab, *Older people and poverty*, © Help the Aged, *Government urged to back 'social tourism'*, © Guardian Newspapers Limited 2005.

Chapter Two: Global Poverty

Global poverty, © NetAid, *Poverty*, © National Youth Agency, *World leaders 'could do more' to tackle poverty*, © Plan-UK, *Natural resources are path out of poverty*, © World Bank, *What do you know?*, © Christian Aid 2005. Used with permission, *Frequently asked questions on world debt*, © Jubilee Debt Campaign, *Millennium Development Goals*, © Oxfam GB, *Millennium Development Goals: poverty and hunger*, © Crown copyright is reproduced with the permission of Her Majesty's Stationery Office, *Poverty and hunger*, © Planet 21, *Trading for justice*, © Save the Children, *Fairtrade takes off in UK*, © Planet 21, *Awareness of Fairtrade*, © MORI, *Voters demand more action on world poverty*, © Oxfam GB, *The rich-poor divide*, © Planet 21, *Children and poverty*, © UNICEF, *Childhood under threat*, © UNICEF, *Cost of school beyond reach of millions*, © Save the Children, *Gender discrimination*, © UNICEF.

Photographs and illustrations:

Pages 1, 14, 25, 30, 34: Simon Kneebone; pages 5, 21: Bev Aisbett; pages 8, 22, 27, 37: Don Hatcher; pages 12, 24, 32, 39: Angelo Madrid.

Craig Donnellan
Cambridge
January, 2006